OUR ISLAND SAINTS

"ANGLES CALL YE THEM?" HE SAID. "NAY, ANGELS RATHER"

OUR ISLAND SAINTS

BY

AMY STEEDMAN

WITH EIGHT DRAWINGS IN COLOUR BY

M. DIBBIN SPOONER

YESTERDAY'S CLASSICS

CHAPEL HILL, NORTH CAROLINA

Cover and arrangement © 2006 Yesterday's Classics.

This edition, first published in 2006 by Yesterday's Classics, is an unabridged republication of the work originally published by T. C. & E. C. Jack, Ltd. in 1912. For a listing of books published by Yesterday's Classics, please visit www.yesterdaysclassics.com. Yesterday's Classics is the publishing arm of the Baldwin Project which presents the complete text of dozens of classic books for children at www.mainlesson.com under the editorship of Lisa M. Ripperton and T. A. Roth.

ISBN-10: 1-59915-031-X

ISBN-13: 978-1-59915-031-4

Yesterday's Classics
PO Box 3418
Chapel Hill, NC 27515

ABOUT THIS BOOK

There was once a child who spent many happy hours in a beautiful garden. She loved to play among the flowers, to stand on tiptoe and look up at the stately white lilies, or bend down to search among the fragrant leaves for sweet-scented violets. Such rare and exquisite flowers blossomed all around her, that it was difficult to decide which was the fairest, and the child used to fancy as she passed along that each one whispered to her "choose me." But she would only shake her head and hurry on, until she reached her own little plot of flowers in a corner of the garden. It was not so sunny or so gay, perhaps, as some of the other flower-beds, but it belonged to her, and that made it beautiful in her eyes.

"It is you I love best, dear flowers," she would say, bending down lovingly over the velvet pansies and sweet pinks, "because you are my very own, and grow in my very own garden."

It is with us, as with that child. We walk through God's garden and look at the fair flowers we call His saints. Although they are all most fair and we love them all, yet we have a special love for those that have lived in our own dear land, because they seem to belong more particularly to ourselves. The saints of every land belong to God; but as He has given us our island home, so we feel that the island saints are our special possession, and like the child we say, "We love you best, dear saints, because you are our very own."

AMY STEEDMAN

EDINBURGH, 1912

CONTENTS

Saint Alban 1

Saint Augustine of Canterbury 11

Saint Kentigern 24

Saint Patrick 45

Saint David 68

Saint Molios 74

Saint Bridget 81

Saint Cuthbert 93

Saint Edward the Confessor 114

Saint Columba 127

Saint Margaret of Scotland 149

Saint Hugh of Lincoln 172

SAINT ALBAN

LONG years ago, when Rome was mistress of the world and her soldiers and citizens were to be found everywhere, even the little island of Britain had its place among the colonies of the great empire. Here the Romans laid their roads and planted their towns, built temples to their gods, and ruled the barbarians with a firm strong hand. Many noble Roman families lived in Britain in those days, and although the life was ruder and rougher than that they were accustomed to in the wonderful city of Rome, still they made their houses as luxurious and comfortable as they could and tried to be content.

It was in one of these well-built houses, with inlaid floors and marble baths, that the little Alban was born, heir to a great Roman family. The parents had settled in the town of Verulam, on the banks of the little river Ver, but they always looked upon Britain as a land of exile, and planned to send their boy back to Rome as soon as he should be old enough to be taught and trained to be a Roman citizen.

But the child himself was very happy in his island home. The little stream that ran past the town was in his eyes a wonderful river which would carry his boats far out to sea. The green hill on the opposite bank was a playground fit for the gods, with its carpet of golden-eyed daisies and yellow buttercups, and the smooth grassy slopes that were so soft to roll upon. The great forests that looked so dark and gloomy held him spell-bound, and he loved to watch the grey mists come rolling over the marshy land, turning everything into a world of mystery.

Never was there a happier child in all the world; but the reason of his happiness was not because he had so many pleasures, but because he was kind and generous to every one round about him. It seemed as if there was a little singing bird in the golden cage of his heart, a bird that was always singing happy songs, and its name was Unselfishness.

Now, as soon as the boy grew old enough, he was sent away to Rome as his parents had planned, for they wished him to learn many things which he could never be taught in the little island of Britain. It seemed to Alban as if he had come to a different world when first he entered the city of Rome. Accustomed as he was to the little town with its few well-built houses, the rude huts and wild marsh wastes, the rolling mists and grey skies, he had never dreamed of such a city as this. Palaces of white marble triumphantly rearing their columns up to heaven; temples of the gods more beautiful than a dream; baths luxurious as those of a king's dwelling; and above all the blue sky, such a blue as he had never even dreamed of, and sunshine which kept him even warmer than his fur coat had ever done.

There was much to learn and much to do in this new world of wonder and magnificence, but as Alban grew into a man, he found that there was something he loved better than all this splendour and luxury. Far away on the banks of the little river, in the island of the mist and grey skies, there was something which bound his heart with a golden thread of love and memory which nothing could snap. Although the house at Verulam was no grand palace; although the country was rough and wild and often cold and bleak, it was home. The great forests, the green flowery hills, the rolling mists seemed to be calling him. It meant home to him, and he loved it better than all the glory of Rome.

So Alban returned to the island of the mists, and lived once more in the house where he was born, on the banks of the little river. He was rich and powerful and had everything that heart could desire, and he was as happy as ever, for he was so kind and generous that every one loved him. Rich and poor alike were welcome at his house, and no one who needed help asked for it in vain. Travellers always stopped at his gate, and he never refused hospitality to any guest.

It was late one night, when doors were barred and every one had gone to rest, that a knocking was heard at the outer gate. It was an urgent knocking although not very loud, and the servants at last went to see who it was that sought shelter at that unseemly hour. A weary-looking man dressed in a long cloak was standing there, and he begged that he might be taken in secretly and hidden from his pursuers, who were even now close at hand.

The servants, knowing their master's will, brought him quickly in, and one went to his lord to tell him of the new arrival. "He hath a strange cloak and seemeth to be a teacher, and one of those whom men call Christians," said the servant, as he told his tale: "he saith that even now he is pursued and hath endured great persecutions."

"See that he is made welcome," said Alban, "and that he is hidden secretly, and let no man prate of his presence here."

The poor hunted man, who was indeed a Christian priest, was brought in and secretly hidden, as Alban had commanded, and for a while his pursuers sought for him in vain.

Alban knew well how cruel were the tortures and punishments which these Christians endured, and he looked to find his guest stricken with terror and fear, but to his surprise the priest's face was calm and even happy.

"Art thou not afraid that thy persecutors may track thee here?" asked Alban curiously.

"My Master is stronger than they," answered the priest calmly. "He will protect me."

"Who is thy master?" asked Alban wonderingly.

"The Lord Christ," answered the priest.

"That poor man who died the death of a criminal?" said Alban, in a mocking voice.

"The King of Heaven, who deigned to come to earth as a helpless child," answered the priest, "and who became Man that He might teach us to be Men."

"And what reward dost thou receive for thy service to this King?" asked Alban, looking at the worn clothes, the weary thin face of the man before him.

"They who serve Christ have no thought of reward," answered the priest. "Their only thought is how much service they may offer their Master. Stripes, persecutions, tortures, death, these are the rewards which His faithful soldiers gladly suffer, that they may be fit to call Him 'Lord.' Wilt thou listen to the story of my King?"

"These are strange sayings of thine," said Alban, "but I will hear no more. 'Tis almost like a call to battle in my ears, and yet I know it is but foolishness. Be silent; I will have no more of thy idle talk."

Disturbed and angry, Alban turned to go, but all that day the words he had heard rang in his ears. How royally was this King served by His followers! Who was He that could command such splendid service? He had heard of this God of the Christians, but had never troubled himself to learn what His life had been.

Then when night came and he lay sleeping, a dream was sent—a dream which told him the story of the King, which he had refused to hear that day. He saw the Man, crowned with the wreath of thorns; he saw the face of majesty and power gazing so pitifully at the cruel throng who seized Him and nailed Him to the cross. He saw the body laid in the tomb, and then the figure of the living Christ ascending with great glory into heaven. And sweeping upwards, there followed a great multitude in white robes, following Him who had conquered death, for whom they too had laid down their lives.

Early next morning Alban went to the secret chamber to seek the priest and ask what that dream could mean.

"God has been very gracious to thee, my son," answered the priest solemnly. "He has taught thee Himself what thou didst refuse to hear from me."

"Tell me more," said Alban humbly; "I will listen to every word that thou canst tell me now."

With a glad heart the priest told over again the story of his Master's life, and Alban listened eagerly. Again the battle-call sounded in his ears, and he longed to serve a Master such as this.

"But hast thou indeed counted the cost of such a service?" asked the teacher. "It is no pleasant service which He offers."

"I seek no pleasant service," answered Alban.

"A cruel death may be thy only reward," said the priest again. "Dost thou not repent the kindness which made thee harbour a Christian?"

"Nay," replied Alban; "thou hast brought me life instead of death. I have never yet repented of one kind or merciful act which I have done to any man."

Then the priest could no longer refuse to baptize the new soldier into the service of the King; but as they knelt in prayer together the servants came hurriedly to the door telling of a band of soldiers who had entered the courtyard and demanded to search the house for the hidden fugitive.

Alban sprang to his feet, and caught up the heavy cloak and cowl of the priest. "Quick! quick!" he cried, "escape thou in my mantle, and I will stay here in thy place. They will scarce discover who I am until thou hast escaped far away out of their reach."

"How can I do this?" said the priest. "Thou wilt suffer in my stead."

" 'Tis my first call to arms," said Alban gladly. "Let me thus begin to serve the King."

There was no time for words; the soldiers were at the door; but when they entered there was but one cloaked figure there, and he showed no resistance, but quietly gave himself into their hands.

The judge was in the temple, sacrificing to his gods, when they brought the fugitive Christian to receive his sentence. And when the cloak was thrown back and he saw the young Roman noble, he was doubly furious because he had been deceived.

"Thou has hidden a traitor in thy house, and well dost thou deserve to bear his punishment," he cried angrily. "Perhaps thou too art a Christian. Sacrifice at once to the gods, and beg for mercy."

"It is as thou sayest; I am a Christian," answered Alban calmly. "I serve the King of Heaven, and will offer no sacrifice to thy false gods."

There was a note of triumph in the voice of the young Roman, and the people wondered when they saw him standing there so fearless and triumphant. Did he not know what it meant to call himself a Christian? He was young and rich and powerful; all the pleasures of life, gay and alluring, lay spread out before him; all the great things which men strive after lay within his grasp; and yet he was choosing torture, dishonour and death. The wondering "why?" was echoed in every heart.

But there was little time for wonder. The soldiers, by order of the judge, seized Alban and dragged him away to be tortured, and then he was led out to be executed in the arena on the opposite side of the river.

All the inhabitants of the town came out to see the sight, and some looked on with pity, remembering the kindness they had received at the hands of the young Roman noble. Others again came out to mock. How gallant and happy he had always looked. There would surely be no smile on his face now! But when they pressed forward, and caught sight of that pale young face, their mocking words were silenced, and a feeling of awe fell upon the crowd. Yes, the old happy look was there still, but there was something higher and purer added to it. A light of wondrous happiness seemed to shine forth, and the people as they looked felt as did those men who gazed upon Saint Stephen. "They saw his face, as it had been the face of an angel."

Down to the little river they led him; but when they came to the bridge there was no room to pass, for the crowd was so great. The order was given to ford the river, but the legend tells us that before Saint Alban could step down, the stream dried up, and he crossed over, without so much as wetting his feet.

Then the old legend goes on to tell how the executioner, who watched this miracle from the opposite bank, was struck with fear and remorse. How could he put to death a man whom heaven itself so carefully guarded? He would not fight against the God of Alban, so he threw down his sword and refused to touch him.

But Alban walked steadfastly on to the place of execution. Up the grassy slopes of the green hill he went, along the flowery path of scented thyme and golden-eyed daisies, where he had loved to play as a little lad. On this bright June day the hill was starred with flowers, and they seemed indeed a fitting carpet to spread beneath the feet of the first English martyr.

There were other executioners ready to do the bidding of the governor, and there, on the green hillside, the first faithful English soldier in the noble army of martyrs laid down his life.

A clear spring of water, it is said, sprang up to mark the spot where Saint Alban was put to death, near the little town of Verulam which now bears his name; but the miracle was scarcely needed. The memory that sprang from the life laid down in merciful kindness for another, in the service of the King, is a spring of living water that can never fail or be cut off.

SAINT AUGUSTINE OF CANTERBURY

THE monk Gregory walked through the market-place of Rome and looked with pitying eyes at the slaves waiting there to be sold like sheep or oxen. It always made him sorrowful and angry to pass through the market and see those poor patient slaves who seemed to have never a friend to help them. It was better perhaps not to pass by that way, and yet the little he could do by friendly words and kindly looks might cheer some of the poor souls, and so the pity that he felt always drew him back.

He knew the market-place so well, and the look of those weary toil-worn faces, and it always seemed to him a very grey sad world in which he walked. But to-day a strange new sight woke him from his half-dreaming pity and made him press forward with eager watchful eyes.

Surrounded by a throng of dark-skinned, brown-eyed Italians there stood a little group of fair-haired children such as Gregory had never seen before. Their limbs were white; their curls shone in the sunlight like threads of gold, and their eyes were as blue as the sky above.

Gregory beckoned to the merchant who stood close by, and pointing to the fair children, asked from whence they came.

"From Britain," answered the man, "where all the people are as fair and beautiful as these are."

"And are they Christians?" asked the monk, with more and more interest.

The merchant shrugged his shoulders and shook his head.

"All heathens," he answered briefly.

"Ah me," sighed Gregory, "to think that so much beauty should belong to the Prince of Darkness; that the souls in such fair bodies should never be visited by God's light."

He turned once more and looked at the boys. "What is the name of their nation?" he asked.

"They are called Angles," replied the merchant.

For a moment a smile lit up the grave face of the monk, the word sounded with such a happy meaning in his ear.

"Angles call ye them?" he said. "Nay, angels rather; for angel-like they are, and must become fit company for angels. But to what province of their country do they belong?"

"Deira," was the answer.

"Ay, and from God's ire they shall be snatched," said Gregory, still playing with the words.

"And the king of the country, how call ye him?"

"Ælla," said the merchant shortly.

"Rightly indeed is your king called Ælla," said Gregory, turning to the wondering boys, "for Alleluia must be chanted in his dominions."

It was an easy matter to buy those fair-haired boys and take them to the convent on the hill, and teach them how to live in the light of God's love. But Gregory wanted more than this. The light must be carried into that far-away land of darkness. His hand was ready to bear the torch, and his heart was filled with an eager longing to be this messenger of light.

Time after time he begged for permission to set out for England, but the Pope and the Roman people had need of his strong arm and wise head, and refused to allow him to leave Rome. At last, however, the Pope secretly and unwillingly gave his consent, and Gregory started off with a few companions and many high hopes. But he did not go far. As soon as it was discovered that their beloved Gregory was gone, the people demanded that he should be recalled, and messengers were sent in haste to fetch him back. He had only gone three days' journey when the messengers overtook him, and so the mission to England came to an end, and with a sorrowful heart Gregory returned to Rome.

But although it was plain that Gregory's work lay in Rome, where ere long he was made Pope, yet he never forgot the great desire of his heart, and never gave up his determination to send the light into that distant land of Britain. So it came to pass that before long he chose out forty monks from his old monastery on the hill and sent them, with Augustine at their head, to the far-away little island which was waiting in darkness for the dawn of God's light.

The monks whom Gregory chose set forth at once as they were bidden, for they had learned above all things to be obedient. But it was a long unknown journey that lay before them, and their hearts were somewhat unwilling and greatly afraid. They started as bravely as they could, but the further they travelled the more troubled they became. People told them the most fearsome tales of the island to which they were bound.

"There is a most terrible sea to cross," said one.

"And even should you escape the fury of the sea, certain death will await you when you arrive," said another.

"Ay," said a third, "for the people are not only heathens but savages, and fierce as wild beasts, and they speak a barbarous language you will never understand."

Sorely disheartened, the monks called a halt, and sent Augustine back to Rome to ask Pope Gregory if they were still to go on in the face of such dangers and difficulties.

It must have been with unwilling feet and a burning heart of shame that Augustine turned back.

He who had been specially chosen by Gregory for this special mission could not have been the kind of man who would be willing to turn his back on any foe or give up the fight without even striking a blow.

The little company of monks waited patiently for the return of their messenger, and ere long he was once more in their midst. The tall figure, "higher than any of the people from his shoulders and upward," stood erect now, and there was a gleam of triumph in his eyes. The order was to march forward, and there was to be no retreat.

"Let not the toil of the journey nor the tongues of evil-speaking men deter you," wrote Gregory, "but with all possible earnestness and zeal perform that which by God's direction you have undertaken."

They needed a strong leader, this little band of despairing monks, and Gregory wisely added in his letter: "When Augustine, your chief, returns, humbly obey him in all things. Had I my wish I would labour with you."

After that there was not one that talked of going back. Not only was obedience the just rule of their order, but the thought that their beloved Gregory would have been with them if he could, made them set their faces steadfastly to do the work which lay before them.

It was truly a terrible journey which they had undertaken. Their path lay through lonely forests and strange countries, where the people often treated them roughly, stoning them and howling after them as they went. Slowly but surely, however, they went their way, and at last reached the sea which swept its angry raging way between them and the grey island of the north. Then with brave hearts they set sail, but as the ship sped on its way and the land they had left grew fainter and fainter in the dim distance, some wondered if they would ever reach the other side, and others were past caring whether they lived or died. Then some one cried aloud that there was land ahead, and eager strained eyes caught sight of a white line upon the horizon, which grew broader and broader until the cliffs of Albion stood out clear against the blue sky, as dazzling in their whiteness as the ramparts of a heavenly city.

But it was with no expectation of finding a heavenly country that the weary band of monks landed at Ebbesfleet, on the Isle of Thanet. Rather they expected at every turn to meet with demons, savage animals, or still more savage people ready to fall upon them and destroy them.

Now the tales which had been told to these poor monks of all the terrors which lurked in wait for them, were much more frightening than true. The Saxon people of Britain were certainly heathens and worshipped strange gods, but they were a brave kindly people, and Ethelbert, the king of that part of the country, was a strong wise man. Already, too, a star of hope had shone out in the heathen darkness if those poor monks had but known it, for Ethelbert's fair Queen Bertha was a Christian, and near the palace, in the tiny chapel of Saint Martin, God was served daily by a faithful priest who had come with the Queen from France.

So instead of fierce blows and savage treatment, instead of being hunted down and driven out as they had expected, the messengers found a peaceful air of welcome and kindliness about this strange land. There was a friendly look in the eyes of the people who watched them pass, and the poor wayfarers thanked God and took fresh courage.

It was in the springtime of the year, when our little grey island forgets her dullness and decks herself in tender green and budding flowers, that Augustine and his monks came to England. There was a feeling of new life and new hope in the air which cheered their hearts, and before long word was brought from the King himself saying he would meet the strangers on the uplands above the sea and hear the message they had brought.

"We will meet in the open air, with the sky above us," said the King. "All shall be open and straight-forward in the light of day."

The royal seat was set upon the green sward of a flowery meadow overlooking the sea, and there the King awaited his curious new guests. Across the April blue of the sky the white clouds scudded in ever-changing shapes. Below the sparkling sea shone like a ring of sapphires round our brave little island. In every sheltered nook and corner the primroses peeped out with their broad sunny faces. Sea-birds swooped and screamed around the white cliffs; all the birds were busy with nest-building; the old magic of spring was awake once more in the land. But there was something even more strange and wonderful than the returning life of spring coming that day to England. Across the bare wind-swept uplands a procession began to move slowly from the seashore. The people watched in breathless silence, wondering what it all might mean. These were no warriors, for they bore no weapons and there was no sign of war. In front, lifted high, a silver cross caught the gleams of sunshine as they came. Then a great picture was carried aloft, the picture of a Man, such as none had ever seen before. Close behind followed a little company of men in dark strange garments, and at their head walked one taller and straighter than all the rest. Slowly the procession went forward, and as the gleaming silver cross moved ever nearer, the sound of a low wailing chant came floating over the land, drowned now and then by the thunder of the waves breaking upon the shore. Nearer and nearer came the procession, and the wailing chant sounded more clearly. Now the watchers heard strange words in an unknown tongue, but they did not guess that the words which those dark-robed figures were chanting were a prayer that God's mercy might save and protect our England.

The King listened with deep attention to all that Augustine had to say. The minutes slipped past into hours, and still the dark-robed monk spoke out his message. Beginning with the birth at Bethlehem, he told the wonderful story of God made Man, coming to dwell amongst us; of His Cross and Passion,

His glorious Resurrection and Ascension, and His call to all men to follow Him.

Then when he had finished there was a silence over all, for the King sat in deep thought, and the people waited for his answer. At last he spoke.

"Truly the words and promises which ye bring me are fair," he said, "but they are new to me and of doubtful authority. I cannot therefore accept them and forsake the religion in which I and all my people have so long believed. But because you are strangers and have come from afar to my country, and as it would seem that ye believe your teaching to be good and excellent, we will not molest you, but rather receive you with kindness and hospitality. Nor do we forbid you to teach and preach your religion."

The King was even better than his word, and the forty monks were given a home to live in, near the palace of Canterbury, and were treated in every way as honoured guests. There they taught and preached to all the people who would listen to them. But there was something besides preaching and teaching which won the hearts of these Saxon people.

The simple, honest, busy lives of the little company of monks, the "silent power of holiness," taught people better than any words what this new service meant. Like the magic touch of spring over the dead land, a new life flowed in, and the first sign of its power was the baptism of the King, when he laid aside his royal robes and took service under his new Master. Before the feast of Christmas came round, ten thousand people were enrolled under the banner of Christ, which had been borne so faithfully by His servant Augustine.

It was good news to send to Gregory, and the monks might well rejoice as they listened to the sound of the Alleluias that echoed now within that heathen land.

But although so much had been done in such a short time, there was ever more and more to do, and the little company of monks, with Augustine at their head, never thought of growing weary or needing rest while so much was still to be accomplished.

Augustine had been commanded by Gregory to return to France and there be consecrated Archbishop; and so the first Archbishop of Canterbury began his work as a prince of the Church and a careful shepherd of his little flock. Many a greeting of encouragement came from Rome, and Pope Gregory sent a most precious gift of a copy of the Holy Bible. It was just one single copy, sent over land and sea to a little island, where God's light had only begun to break dimly through the clouds of heathen darkness, and yet it was the seed from which has sprung the glory and honour of our England.

Slowly but surely the monks worked on, building their churches and carrying their torch further and further into the darkness. King Ethelbert, "noble and valiant" as his name signified, was no half-hearted soldier of Christ, and in simple loyalty he gave up his own royal palace at Canterbury for the monks who were doing God's work in his kingdom. With such an example before them, it was little wonder that the people as well pressed forward to help in the work. It is said, too, that many miracles were performed by these simple faithful monks; many sick folk were healed, and wonders were worked as in the days of the Apostles.

But it was not only the monks who went out to work. Augustine, the Archbishop, would never consent to stay safely at home, but was always the first to undertake fresh journeys and risk new dangers. In his simple monk's robe, unarmed and on foot, he went with his brethren from north to south, from east to west, preaching and teaching through the length and breadth of England. Sometimes they met with harsh treatment; showers of stones, and even sharp weapons were used against them, but no serious hurt ever befell the little band of brave men.

Now among the wild mountains of Wales there were still many of the early British Christians who had been driven there by the conquering Saxons. Augustine was very anxious that these men should join with him now and help to make the whole land Christian. But these poor men hated the Saxons, who had driven them from their home and conquered their land. It seemed almost too much to expect them to return good for so much evil. However, they agreed to meet Augustine and his monks and talk the matter over. They fixed the meeting-place on the border of Wales, and there, under a great oak tree, the stranger Archbishop from Rome, and the hunted bishops and monks of the ancient British Church, met.

They talked long and earnestly, and at one time it seemed as if Augustine would persuade them to help him in his work. But those British Christians were very bitter in their dislike to their Saxon conquerors, and they mistrusted a stranger monk who called himself Archbishop of Canterbury. They scarcely knew what to decide, but took counsel with an old hermit who lived a holy life among the wild mountains of Wales.

"Is it our duty to make friends with this man?" they asked.

"If he is a man of God, then follow him," replied the hermit.

"But how are we to know if he be a man of God?" they asked.

"If he be meek and lowly, he bears the yoke of Christ, and offers the same to you," was the answer. "But if he be proud and haughty he cannot be of God."

"How are we to judge whether he be meek and lowly or proud and haughty?" they asked again.

"Contrive it thus," said the hermit. "See that this man and his company arrive first at the meeting-place, so that he may be seated ere you come. If he shall arise and greet you, be sure he is Christ's servant. But if he despises you, and does not rise at your coming, then you may in turn despise him."

The plan was easily carried out. The great oak tree spread its branches over Augustine's little company as they rested there, waiting for the coming of the men who had promised to meet them there. Augustine, weary and anxious, sat in his seat gazing out with thoughtful, troubled eyes which saw no fair green meadows or pleasant landscape, but only dark clouds of distrust and enmity. So when at last the company of British priests drew near, the tall figure dreaming his dreams sat on motionless in his seat, and made no movement to rise or come forward to greet them.

Half triumphantly, then, those men of the ancient British Church decided that Augustine was no servant of God, and they refused to have aught to do with him.

So Augustine went back to his work alone, and it is to him and his little band of faithful monks that England owes her great debt of gratitude. Long and patiently he worked, never sparing himself, and well had he earned his rest when they laid him in his quiet grave in the church at Canterbury, which he himself had built. We know little of Augustine; he was but a messenger sent by the great Gregory who had planned the mission to England. But to us the man who carried out the plan, the messenger who brought the message, the hand that bore the torch, is worthy of a special love and honour. Like that other messenger, Saint John the Baptist, sent by God, he desired no honour for himself, but was content to be a voice crying in the wilderness, "Prepare ye the way of the Lord; make His paths straight."

SAINT KENTIGERN

THE night was dark, and never a star shone in the blackness of the sky. The wind howled as it swept across the troubled waters of the Firth of Forth, and there was no light on sea or land to guide any belated fishing-boat to a safe haven. It would have been a difficult and dangerous task for any sailor to steer his boat on such a night, and yet the one frail little barque that was tossing about in the stormy waters made its way surely and steadily towards the land.

It was indeed but a frail little boat that so gallantly held its way. Over the framework of wooden laths was stretched a covering of hides, scarcely strong enough to withstand the lash of the waves. There were no oars and no rudder, and the boat seemed empty save for a dark form that crouched at the bottom with white upturned face.

But though there was no one to guide the boat, still it went steadily onward, rising like a cork over the crests of the threatening waves, so that scarce a drop of their spray fell upon the dark figure that clung there so desperately.

Presently there was a grating sound, and then a wild sweep upward, as the boat was lifted on the crest of a wave and dashed high and dry upon a sandy shore, while the sea sank sullenly back. Then the dark figure rose quickly, and tried to peer with her wild sad eyes into the blackness around. She was but a maiden yet, and very beautiful, but her beauty was dimmed by the look of suffering and weariness that had paled her cheek and dulled her eyes. A king's daughter this, driven out by cruel hands, but carried by the pitiful waves to a safe haven.

All was very black and very still as the maiden gazed around, but presently a tiny glow of light showed through the darkness, and, stumbling as she went, she managed to reach the place where a few dying embers in a circle of rude stones marked the spot where some shepherds had left their fire to die out.

With a sob of thankfulness the tired traveller knelt and, with trembling breath, coaxed the ashes into a glow, and gathered some of the sticks that were scattered around to lay upon the embers. How good it was to feel the warmth stealing through her stiff frozen limbs; how comforting to see the merry little red tongues of flame lighting up the darkness that was so lonely and so terrible!

But another light had now begun to melt the darkness of the night. Far away in the east the long-looked-for dawn was lifting with its rosy finger the grey curtain of morning twilight. And with the light there came to the lonely maiden by the little fire, the light and joy of her life—her baby son, sent by God to comfort her. Poor little wailing child, he had but a cold welcome to this world of ours. There was no roof to cover him, no soft garments to enfold him; only his mother's arms to wrap him round, only the little red fire to warm him and bid him welcome.

It was thus that another Baby had come to earth in the stable at Bethlehem long ago, and this little one too, like the King of Heaven, found friends among the kindly shepherd folk. Not far off from the sandy beach the shepherds had been herding their flocks, and as they looked seaward in the dim light of dawn, they saw a thin curl of blue smoke rising from the shore. Surely, then, their fire had not died out, and it would be good to warm themselves in the chill morning air. They were rough strong men these shepherds, accustomed to a rough rude life, but when they came to the sandy beach and saw the poor young mother with her little newborn son, like the shepherds of old they too knelt down in reverence and with tender hands wrapped their warm coats about the mother and child, and brought out their poor breakfast, offering all that they had.

"We must away and tell the good Saint Servanus," said one. "He will care for these poor strangers."

"Hasten, then," cried another, "and we will follow on and gently bear the mother and her little one to the dwelling of the saint."

So it was arranged, and two of the younger shepherds started in hot haste to tell the good saint of the adventure that had befallen them. They knew that they would find him ready to listen to their story, for he ever rose with the dawn to offer his daily service to God.

"Father, father," they cried, as the old man came forth from the little church to meet them. "We have a strange thing to tell thee. On the shore of Culross we have but now found a fair young maiden with her newborn son. The child was born at dawn of day, and we would know if we may bring them both hither to thee."

A wonderful light shone on the face of the old man as he listened to the words. A child born at the dawn of day! Why, that must have been the meaning of the angel's song which had fallen on his wondering ears as he knelt before the altar! His heart had been lifted up in prayer when the song "Gloria in Excelsis" came floating down, and he waited for some sign to show what it all should mean.

Scarcely had the breathless shepherds finished their tale when the others followed on, one gently bearing the weary mother, while the other tenderly held the tiny babe in a fold of his cloak.

The old saint hurried forward with eager steps and held out his trembling hands to take the child.

"My dear one, my dear one," he cried, "blessed art thou that hast come in the name of the Lord."

So the old saint took the child to his heart. The echo of the heavenly voices still rang in his ears, and he felt sure that this little child sent to earth at the dawn of light would be one of the heralds of the True Light that had come into the world.

When a few days had passed and the poor mother had poured her sad tale into his kindly ears, Saint Servanus brought the maiden and her child to the font of the little church, and baptized the mother by the name of Thenew. Then he took the baby in his arms and poured the water over its little downy head, giving him the name of Kentigern. But there was another name by which the child was often called, Mungo, or "dear one," the name used by the old man that early morning when he took the little one into his arms and into his heart.

Under the care of the good saint the child grew into a strong brave boy. He had no lack of companions, for many boys were gathered at the monastery to be taught and trained by the learned Saint Servanus. With them he learned his lessons and played his games, but, although he was kind and generous, the boys did not greatly love him. It was not so much that they envied his quickness at lessons, or his beautiful voice which soared above all the rest in the daily hymn of praise: this they might have suffered, but they felt sure that the master loved him best, and this was more than they could bear. They began to wish with all their hearts that Kentigern would be tempted to do some mean evil deed and thus lose favour in the eyes of the old man, who took such a pride in his goodness and cleverness.

The saints of God have always had a special love for His dumb creatures, and have treated both birds and beasts with tender care. The blessed Saint Francis was never so happy as when among his "little sisters the birds," while all animals came to him at his call as if to a friend. Saint Servanus too had his favourite "little sister," a tiny robin-redbreast, so tame that it would come and perch on the old man's shoulder, hop upon his hand, and at matins would cheerfully chirp its little hymn of praise with the rest. It was so small and trustful, so sure of its welcome when it came hopping down, cocking its head on one side and looking at him with its bright eye, that the saint would smile and call it his spoilt child. Before eating his own meals the "little sister" had first her share.

Now the boys who were so jealous of Kentigern were inclined to hate the poor little robin too. Many a time had the master bade them take a lesson from his little favourite, mark its prompt obedience in coming at once when it was called, watch its busy ways, and note how cheerful was its song of praise. They answered never a word, but in their hearts they thought it was by no means pleasant to be sent to learn lessons from a silly little bird.

So the evil feeling grew until at last one night, when the saint had gone into the church alone, they found the redbreast chirping away on a branch outside the door, and, as it was so tame, they caught it with the greatest ease. At first they did not mean to harm it, only to frighten it a little, but their ways were rough, and ere long they took to quarrelling as to who should hold it, and began to snatch it from each other's grasp. Then before they half realised what they had done, the poor little bird lay dead in their hands, its feathers all torn and ruffled, its bright eyes closed, its head hanging limp and still. A dreadful hush fell on the noisy throng as they looked at their work.

"Oh! what will the master say?" cried one.

"We dare not tell him," said another.

"He will know without any telling," said a third.

"Oh! how we shall be whipped," wailed all the rest in chorus.

A shiver went round at the words. Each one knew exactly how that whipping would smart, and almost felt it already.

"Here comes the good boy Kentigern," cried another; "he of course is safe from blame, just as he always is."

The boys looked at one another. The same thought had struck them all. Why not put the blame on Kentigern and say that he had killed the bird? Would that not serve two good ends? They would be saved from the master's wrath and that most certain whipping, and Kentigern would be humbled and cast out of favour.

Even as they hurriedly agreed to this plan, the church door opened and the saint came forth. His keen eye saw at once that something was wrong. The crowd of silent boys were all looking expectantly towards him, and in their midst stood Kentigern bending over something which he held in his hand.

"What mishap has befallen?" asked the old man, gazing at the eager faces.

"It is Kentigern," they cried with one voice all together. "He has killed thy little bird."

The master said nothing, but looked at the silent figure bending over the little bunch of ruffled feathers. Kentigern did not seem to hear or to heed the loud accusation. Very gently he stroked the feathers and laid his cheek against the tiny body that was still warm. Then he knelt down, and, raising one hand, made the sign of the cross over the bird.

"Lord Jesus Christ," he prayed, "in whose hands is the breath of every creature, give back to this bird the breath of life, that Thy blessed name may be glorified for ever." And as he prayed there was a faint stirring among the feathers, a ruffling of the wings, and the robin flew to its safe shelter on the shoulder of the master. Now the old chronicle which tells this tale does not add whether the boys received the whipping which they had feared, but we trust that their forebodings were smartly realised. If so, it may have taught them to treat God's creatures more gently, but it certainly did not cure them of the sin of envy and jealousy, for Kentigern continued to have but a hard time amongst them.

It was the rule of Saint Servanus that each of the boys should in turn take charge of the lighting of the sanctuary lamps. Thus the boy whose turn it was to see that the lamps were trimmed and lighted was obliged to keep up the fires while all the rest were in bed, so that there should not fail to be a spark ready to kindle light for the early service. When it fell to Kentigern's turn, the boys thought of a fresh plan to bring disgrace upon his head.

As soon as all the fires had been carefully made up, and Kentigern had gone to rest, the other boys crept silently out of bed and went the round of the monastery, raking out every fire. Not a spark did they leave that could light a single lamp, and then they went joyfully back to bed, feeling well satisfied with their work.

At cockcrow Kentigern rose as usual to go and make ready for the early service, but he found every fire black and dead. Search as he might, there was no means of kindling a light, although he had built up each fire carefully to last until morning.

Then the boy's heart was full of anger. All the wrongs he had suffered patiently, all the unkind tricks of the other boys rose up in his memory, and he felt that he could bear it no longer. It was all so mean and underhand. They did not dare stand up and openly defy him, for they knew he was brave and fearless, but in the dark they plotted and planned how they might punish and disgrace him. No; he would stand it no longer; he would leave the monastery and make his own way in the world.

So forth he went, swinging along with great angry strides until he came to the hedge that bounded the monastery lands. By this time his anger had begun to cool and leave room for other thoughts. After all it was rather cowardly to run away, even from injustice and persecution, for it meant also running away from duty and the good old man who was like a father to him. What would the master say when he entered the church and found it in darkness, the altar lights unlit, the lamps untended?

Very slowly, then, Kentigern retraced his steps, holding in his hand the hazel twig which he had broken off from the hedge when he stood debating which road to take. He was thinking deeply as he walked, and it suddenly flashed across his mind that there was a way of obtaining the light he needed which as yet he had not tried. Surely God would not fail to help him. So, just as he had prayed in faith over the dead bird, he knelt down on the dewy grass and, making the holy sign over the little twig, prayed God to kindle in it a living spark that might light the lamps for His service. The legend tells us that as he prayed God did indeed send down fire that lit into a tiny torch the hazel twig, and that it burnt steadily until all the lamps in the church were lit, one by one.

Again there is no mention of the whipping which those boys deserved, but Kentigern was no tale-bearer, and this his enemies knew full well.

So time went on, and Kentigern grew into a tall lad, the comfort and joy of his master. He was almost a man now, and it was time that he should leave the monastery and his sheltered life there, and find his own work in the world.

HE KNELT DOWN ON THE DEWY GRASS

Not in anger this time did he plan his departure, but with a humble heart, and he prayed to God for guidance. Not only was he the cause of much quarrelling and jealousy among the rest, but, what was even worse, people had begun to praise and flatter him and call him a wonderful boy, and he felt sure that it was time he should go. So he made up his mind to leave the monastery, and early one morning, after his work was done, he started forth.

It was to the river that Kentigern bent his steps, scarcely knowing which way to turn, but drawn to the place where the shepherds' fire had warmed him as a tiny baby, where the cry of the seabirds and the moan of the sea had drowned his first feeble wail. Journeying on and on by the side of the winding Forth, he reached at last a place where a bridge spanned the silver river. The water was flowing quietly beneath him as he crossed the bridge, but when he had reached the other side it rose higher and higher in a great spate until the bridge was entirely swamped. Then, as Kentigern stood and watched the furious torrent, he saw his old master on the opposite bank, leaning with one hand upon his staff and with the other beckoning him to return. The aged saint had followed him all the long way from the monastery, and his voice came sounding mournfully across the rushing waters.

"Alas, my son, light of my eyes, staff of my old age, wherefore dost thou leave me?"

"My father," cried Kentigern, "it grieves me sorely, but I must go forth to my work. Thou knowest that as truly as I do."

"Then let me come with thee, my son," cried the old man. "Thou hast been mine since the day when the angels sang of thy birth, and the shepherds placed thee in my arms."

"I know it," said the boy, and he stretched out his arms with a loving gesture towards the old man, "but I must go forth, and my work lies yonder, while thy work lies behind. Fare thee well, and God guard and keep thee until the time when He shall take thee home."

Saint Servanus knew that the boy was right, and that he must finish his life-work alone, while the strong young lad, the herald of the dawn, should carry the light into the dark places of the land. Sorrowfully, then, he returned to the monastery, and Kentigern journeyed on alone.

For a while Kentigern lived and worked at Camock, but as the years went by, the fame of his holy life and the good deeds which he did reached the ears of the king of that country.

The Church was then in evil plight, for although the people had been taught the true religion in days gone by, they had sadly lapsed, and many had learned to worship idols and believe in strange gods, as did the pagans who had invaded their land.

The King and the clergy, therefore, of the Cambrian region sought to strengthen and fortify the

Church, and what better weapon could they find for their purpose than this wonderful young man, whose influence over people was so marvellous and who lived such a pure and blameless life?

But when they came to tell Kentigern that they had decided to make him a bishop, he was amazed and dismayed.

"I am too young," he said.

"Thy ways are staid, and thou hast much learning," they answered.

"It would take me from my prayers and meditations," urged Kentigern.

"There are other souls to be saved besides thine own," they gravely answered.

Then Kentigern bowed his head, and said sadly, "But I am not worthy"; and they answered, "Because thou thinkest thyself unworthy, we are all the more certain that thou art the one man we seek."

There was more talk after this, and at last Kentigern saw that there was no other way but to accept the post of honour and difficulty. A bishop from Ireland was ready to consecrate him to his high office, and he was made Bishop of Glesgu, a little place on the banks of the Clyde. There a wattled church was built and a fortified monastery, and there, in the midst of a wild country and a still wilder people, Kentigern began his rule. Little by little, houses were built close around the church and monastery until a village was formed. Then the village became a town, and as the years rolled by the town grew into the great city of Glasgow.

But in the days of Saint Kentigern Glesgu meant only "the dear family," for so the saint named the little gathering of God's servants who dwelt together under one rule and had all things in common, seeking only to do God's service.

There was no jealousy or ill-feeling now for Kentigern to fight against, for the brethren all loved their bishop and obeyed him as their master. But it was no life of ease to which he was called, but one of difficulty, hardship, and strenuous work. Early in the morning he rose from his bed, which boasted no soft pillow nor warm covering, and however cold the morning, he plunged into the river close by to brace his body for his day's work. The clothes he wore were rough and coarse below, but above he wore a pure white alb or cloak and the stole of his office over his shoulder. And well might the white folds of his mantle be to men a sign of the pure childlike soul that dwelt in the strong man's body.

It is said that, as he knelt before the altar, the prayers which rose from "the golden censer of his heart" seemed to reach to the very gates of heaven, for often as the faithful people knelt around him they saw a white dove with a golden beak descend and hover above his head, overshadowing with its snowy wings the altar and the kneeling bishop.

There was little rest for the servants of God in those days. Far and near they journeyed among the people scattered around the wild countryside. However far the journey, Kentigern always went on foot, and there was no hardship which he shrank from enduring if he could but bring one lost sheep back into the fold. Preaching, teaching, building churches, strengthening and leading back those that had wandered from the True Light, his work went on from day to day.

But once in the year, when the season of Lent came round, Kentigern left his brethren and went to dwell alone in a far-off cave. It was the time when our Lord had gone into the wilderness to wrestle with the tempter, and well did Kentigern know how blessed it was to be alone with God.

In the lonely cave there was nothing to chain his thoughts to earth and men. The song of the birds, the rippling laughter of the burns unlocked from their winter bonds of ice, the little grey furry caps of the willow buds, the soft green of the sprouting grass, everything fitted in with the praise and prayer which filled his days.

Then when Good Friday came he returned to his brethren, wan and wasted indeed with fasting, but with a face that seemed to reflect the light of heaven, so near to its gates had he dwelt.

But although Kentigern fasted and endured many hardships, he had always a happy cheerful face, and he had no belief in gloomy looks. Often he would tell his brethren that what he disliked above all was a hypocrite who went about sighing with eyes cast down and a long face. They seemed, he said, to think they were walking after the manner of turtledoves, whereas in reality it was the peacock they resembled. And what was the use of looking down on the dust when eyes might be lifted to heaven? No, hypocrisy was one of the little foxes that spoiled the grapes, and God loved those who did their work with a cheerful countenance and simplicity of heart.

So many years passed away and then evil times befell the "dear family" at Glesgu. Another king now reigned, one who hated the Church and talked with scornful contempt of the bishop and his workers. The seasons, too, had been bad and the harvest poor, and Kentigern found that there was no corn to feed the brethren nor to give to the poor who came to him for aid.

It was surely the duty of the King to help his people, so the bishop went boldly to the court and asked that out of his abundance the King would spare corn for his hungry people.

The King laughed aloud at the request and answered with mocking words.

"Thou who teachest others to cast their burden upon the Lord, should surely practise thyself the same. How is it that thou who fearest God art poor and hungry, while I, who have never sought the kingdom of heaven, have all things I can desire, and Plenty smileth upon me? Therefore what thou preachest is a lie."

Calmly then did Kentigern make answer that God has often seen fit to afflict the just and allow the wicked to flourish like a green bay tree.

This enraged the King still further, and he bade Kentigern work a miracle if he could.

"If, without the aid of human hands and trusting only in thy God, thou canst transfer to thy house all the grain that is in my barns, I will yield it to thee as a gift," he said, with a mocking laugh.

Kentigern left the King, carrying with him an anxious heavy heart. There were so many hungry mouths to fill and all depended upon him. But not for a moment did he lose his faith in the goodness of God, and he prayed earnestly to Him that the daily bread might be provided.

That very night a great storm came sweeping down the river and the waters began to rise. Higher and higher swelled the torrent until it overflowed the river bank, and swirling round the King's barns, it lifted them bodily from the ground and carried them out on to the river. There the current caught them and swept them along till they reached the place where Kentigern dwelt, where it left them high and dry, with not so much as a grain of corn spoilt by the water. So God took the King's gift to feed His people.

The mocking King was filled with fury when he learned what had happened, and so cruel became his persecution of Kentigern and his brethren, that they at last determined to leave the monastery and to seek afar off some place where they might dwell in peace.

Travelling southward, Kentigern dwelt some time in Cumberland, where, as was his custom wherever he rested, he erected a stone cross, as a sign of his faith, at a little place still known as Crossfell. Then, travelling on by the seashore, he sought in the wild country for some convenient place where he might found another home.

There is a legend that tells of a white boar that guided him, but it was more likely a kindly stream like his own river Clyde which led him by its silver thread to a place which seemed all that he could wish.

They were no mere dreamers these monks of old, and they did not look for miracles to work for them when the work could be done with their own hands. The wilderness was soon humming as with a hive of bees, and in a wonderfully short space of time trees were cut down, fashioned into beams, fitted together, and a great wooden church and monastery was built to the glory of God.

But it seemed as if Kentigern was never to be free from persecution, for scarcely was the monastery finished when the prince of North Britain came riding through the forest with his followers, and demanded what these strangers meant by settling on his land.

In vain did Kentigern answer peaceably. The prince would not be appeased, and in his anger he threatened to pull down the church and chase the builders off the land.

Then a strange thing happened, for suddenly the light of day faded from the eyes of the angry man and black darkness came swiftly over him.

"What is this?" he cried, staggering forward, stretching out helpless groping hands. "The light is gone. I can see nothing."

In haste his men came crowding round and lifted him up, but they saw at once that he was blind and they knew not what to do.

"Bring him hither to me," said Kentigern, and the men led him forward, guiding his stumbling steps.

The heart of the good bishop was touched by the sight of the helpless man, and he earnestly prayed to God that He would lighten the darkness and restore sight to those dull eyes. Even as he prayed the light returned, and the grateful prince knelt at the feet of the saint and kissed the hem of his robe in reverence and thankfulness.

There was no more talk of pulling down the church or chasing the brethren, but the prince humbly sat at Kentigern's feet to be taught to know the True Light which alone could lighten the darkness of his mind.

So things prospered greatly at the new monastery, which grew even greater and more powerful than the old home at Glesgu. But just as Kentigern was beginning to dream of a rest in his old age and thought to end his days in his peaceful new home, he was called once again to fresh labours.

A new king had come to reign over the Cambrian kingdom; one who loved the Church, and strove to establish it once more in his kingdom.

Surely, then, the first thing to be done was to send for the good bishop and bid the shepherd return to gather together his flock once more in the old home at Glesgu.

It was hard to leave the home he had made and begin all over again the old work and struggle, but Kentigern never hesitated. The new monastery was left under the care of a faithful brother, Saint Asaph, and Kentigern once more turned his face northwards and returned to his native land.

Many years he laboured, and with him returned peace and prosperity, for the brethren were busy skilled workers, and they taught the people to work the land to the best advantage. The King, too, put all things in his kingdom under the rule of the wise bishop, so that his word was law throughout the country. And it is said that the holy Saint Columba journeyed from his island home to greet the saint whose fame had spread even as far as Iona.

So the herald of the dawn did indeed bring light into the dark places of his beloved land, and when his work was done on the morn of the Epiphany, when the silver lamp of the morning star was paling in the light of the coming dawn, the angels came to carry home the soul of him at whose birth they had sung their "Gloria in Excelsis." And surely now their song must have risen in still higher triumph, for his warfare was accomplished, the work of the weary old man was finished, and behold, his soul was still as the soul of a little child!

SAINT PATRICK

IT was a dark night of storm and wind, but the people in the little farm on the western coast of Scotland were accustomed to stormy winds and the sound of breakers dashing upon the rocky shore, and they paid little heed to the wintry weather. They were all tired out with their day's work, and thankful, when the darkness closed in, to bar the doors and shut out the wild night as they gathered round the fire within. A rough set of people they looked in the light of the great peat fire that burned on the hearth. Only one, a boy of sixteen, seemed different to the rest, and had a gentler, more civilised look, while he held himself as if accustomed to command.

This boy was Patrick, son of the master Calponius, who belonged to the Roman colony at Dumbarton, and he had been brought up with care and taught all that a young Roman citizen should know. His gentle mother, niece of the holy Saint Martin of Tours, had brought with her many a cherished memory of courtly manners from the sunny land of her birth, and she had taught the boy to be courteous and knightly in his bearing. So it was that Patrick learned many things which were as yet unknown in the savage northern land where he dwelt, but chiefest among all was the faith of Christ, taught to him by his father and mother, who were both Christians.

But all these lessons seemed very dull and uninteresting to the restless boy. It was such a waste of the golden hours to sit indoors and learn those endless psalms. Prayers, too, took such a weary time, when he might be out on the hillside, as free as the happy birds and all the wild creatures that lived under the open sky. Sometimes in his heart he almost wondered whether it might not be pleasanter to be a heathen rather than a Christian. The heathen had no psalms to learn and could do just as they pleased.

"Some day thou wilt grow wiser," said his mother, "and what is but a dull lesson to thee now will be like apples of gold in pictures of silver."

But Patrick could not understand what she meant, and he was only too glad when lesson-time was over and he was allowed to go off to the little farm close to the sea, where he could work with his hands and not with his head. How he loved the rough free life there; the days spent in the fields and woods, the evenings when the peat was heaped high on the glowing hearth, and he listened to the stories of brave deeds and wild adventures which were told or sung in the flickering firelight! What cared he for shrieking winds and the roar of the breakers outside? It was fitting music to echo around the splendid tales that made his heart beat like a drum and his eyes glow like the fire.

"It is a wild night," said one of the men, "and black as the pit. We must needs have a wild song to match the night and chase away the blackness."

So the rude chant of savage deeds and wild adventures was taken up one by one, until the roar of the storm was drowned in their ears and the wail of the wind became part of the mournful music.

But outside in the blackness the wind had sterner work to do than to act as chorus to idle tales. What were those mysterious long black boats that fought their way so stubbornly through the angry waves? They seemed like phantoms of the night, so silently they moved, showing never a glimmer of light from stem to stern. In vain the icy wind swept down upon them and strove to beat them back. Slowly but surely they crept on until they reached a sheltered bay where sand was smooth and it was safe to land.

Black and silent as their boats the pirate crew landed one by one, and, like the ghosts of sea-monsters, crawled stealthily over the rocks and up the hill towards the farm that nestled in a hollow there. The light from the peat fire shone through the little window; a burst of wild song came floating out into the dark night: there was no thought of lurking danger or surprise.

Closer and closer crept the black figures until they too could listen to the story that was chanted by the fireside, and they laughed aloud to hear such brave words coming from the lips of men who sat safe and warm within, little dreaming of the real danger that beset them without.

"Hark!" cried one of the singers suddenly, "surely the wind hath a strange voice to-night. To me it soundeth like the laughter of demons."

With one accord the company started to their feet, for the sound they heard was no voice of the storm. The door was burst inwards with a tremendous crash, and well might the little company think for a moment that demons were abroad. Fearlessly and bravely they fought, but one by one they were overpowered, and either killed outright or bound hand and foot. The captain stood and looked at the row of sullen captives.

"Away with them to the boats," he cried. Then, pointing to Patrick, he added, "See that ye handle that one carefully, for he is a strong lad and will fetch a good price when we land on the other side."

There was nothing to be done, no rescue to hope for, and resistance only made matters worse. Patrick lay stunned and despairing in the bottom of the boat which was to carry him away from his home and his friends. It was all like a bad dream, the tossing of that stormy sea, the long dark night, the landing in a strange country, and the knowledge that he was now a slave to be sold to the highest bidder.

So Patrick came to Ireland, and was sold to a man whom they called Michu, and sent out into the fields to feed his master's swine.

SAINT PATRICK

Strong and hardy as the boy was, the life which he had now to lead taxed his endurance to the uttermost. There was little rest or leisure, for a slave's work is never finished, and he was often so hungry and so bitterly cold that he felt half stunned with misery. Even when the snow was on the ground he had to drive out his herd of pigs to find food for them, and often he was out all night upon the hillside, sheltering in some rocky corner as best he could from the biting wind that swept over the mountains.

In those long dark nights there was plenty of time for thinking, and the boy's thoughts were always of the far-off home and all that he had lost. Strangely enough it was not of the happy careless hours that he dreamed, but rather of the times that had once seemed so tiresome and so long. He loved to think of his mother, and those dull lessons which had once made him so impatient. Little by little all that he had learned came back to him, but instead of being only tiresome lessons, the psalms and prayers held a curious comforting message, as if a friend were speaking to him. Then their meaning became clearer and clearer until he realised that they were indeed a message from a real Friend. Though he was alone, homeless and utterly friendless, God was still there.

"Our Father," said the boy to himself, and the very words seemed to change everything around. God was here in this terrible unknown country, and God was his Father. To be a slave lost half its bitterness when he could stand upright and know himself to be God's servant as well.

For six long years Patrick served his master, Michu, diligently and well, for all this time he was learning also to serve God. With that love in his heart, he learned to care for all helpless things, and to see what was beautiful in common things around. Years afterwards, when he was a great teacher and the heathen priests scoffed at his teaching, and asked how he could explain the Trinity "Three Persons in One God," Patrick stooped down and plucked a leaf of the little green shamrock, which had taught him one of his lessons on the lonely hillside, and, showing its three leaves in one, gave a simple illustration of the great Mystery.

It was at the end of his sixth year of slavery, that one night Patrick drove his pigs to a distant hill overlooking his master's farm, and there, under the stars, in the shelter of a rock, he lay down to rest. It was not long before he fell asleep; but in his sleep he heard a voice close at hand speaking to him.

"Thy fasting is well," said the voice; "thou shalt soon return to thy country. Behold a ship is ready for thee, but thou must journey many miles."

Patrick started up, never doubting for a moment but that this was the message of an angel. He had lived so close to God that he was ever ready to receive His commands. In the story of his life, which he has written himself, he says, "I went in the power of the Lord, who directed my way for good, and I feared nothing until I arrived at that ship."

Weary, footsore, and worn after the long journey on foot, Patrick presented himself before the ship's captain, and prayed that he might be taken aboard and carried over to Britain. It was perhaps small wonder that the captain looked with suspicion at the wild figure of the runaway slave, and bade him angrily begone.

It was a bitter ending to Patrick's hopes, and he turned very sorrowfully away. The journey had been so long, and he had felt so sure that all would be well at the end. Then, as ever, his first thought was to turn to his One Friend, and so he knelt down on the shore and prayed for help and guidance. The answer came even as he prayed, and he heard a shout from one of the sailors, who had followed him.

"Come along," he cried, "they are asking for thee."

Back went Patrick in all haste, and found that meanwhile the captain had changed his mind.

"Come, we will take thee on trust," he said, meaning that Patrick should work out his own passage, or repay him when they landed. "We are about to sail, and hope to reach land in three days."

Those were three days of great happiness to Patrick, as he saw Ireland growing fainter and fainter in the distance, and knew that before him lay freedom and home, and all that he had lost.

But although the ship reached land in three days, it was not the land he knew, and he was still far off from home. The crew of the ship landed somewhere on the coast of Brittany, and tried to find their way to some town, having to travel across a strange, desolate country where there were no inhabitants and nothing to guide them. Day by day their store of food grew less, until they had nothing left to eat, and it seemed as if they must die of starvation.

Now the captain had found that Patrick was to be trusted, and had watched him often at his prayers, and came to think there must be some truth in a religion that made a man so honest and ready to do his duty. So now he called Patrick to him to ask his advice.

"Christian," he said, "thy God is powerful; pray for us, for we are starving."

"I will pray," answered Patrick, "but thou too must have faith in the Lord."

So just as a hungry child turns to his father and asks for bread, Patrick knelt and prayed to God, and suddenly there was a sound of rushing and tearing through the wood, and a herd of wild boars came sweeping along. The men gave chase, and soon captured and killed enough to provide food for many days.

After many adventures Patrick at last reached home, and for a while forgot all the hardships he had endured in the joy and happiness of that wonderful home-coming.

But the careless happy days of boyhood were over now, and a man's work was waiting for him.

SAINT PATRICK

"Only let the work be here," prayed his mother. "O my son, promise that thou wilt never leave us again, now that we have so wonderfully found thee."

For a while that too was Patrick's only wish, never to leave the dear home and those he loved so well.

But, as he lay asleep one night, the heavenly messenger came once more to him and pointed out the path which God would have him tread. It seemed to Patrick that the angel held in his hand a bundle of letters, and on one was written "the voice of the Irish." This he gave to Patrick, who, as he read, seemed to hear the call of many voices echoing from the land where he had been a slave. Even the voices of little children rang in his ears, and all of them were calling to him and saying, "We entreat thee, come and walk still in the midst of us."

The thought of those poor untaught people who had never heard of God had often made him long to help them, and this call decided him. He would enter God's service as a priest, and then go back to the country of his captivity to carry the torch of God's love in his hand, and spread abroad the glorious light in every corner of the dark land.

After a long time of preparation and study, Patrick was at last consecrated bishop, and then set out at once to return to the country where he had suffered so much.

It was a very different coming this time to the arrival of the boy-slave many years before. With his train of clergy and helpers, the bishop, pastoral staff in hand, landed on the sandy shore of Strangford Lough, and he bore himself as a conqueror marching to victory.

Strangely enough, the first person to greet the band of strangers was a swineherd guarding his pigs, just as Patrick had done in those long years of slavery. The lad was terrified when he saw these strange men, and although Patrick spoke kindly to him in his own tongue, the swineherd fled away to the woods. With all haste he returned to his master, Dichu, and told his news.

"There are pirates landing at the bay," he cried, "strange men who come to rob and kill."

Dichu in alarm immediately armed himself and his followers and set out to meet the enemy. But instead of the savage pirates he expected, he found a band of peaceful unarmed men, with one at their head whom it was easy to see was no robber.

Patrick came forward then to meet the chief, and the two men talked a while earnestly together.

"Put up your weapons," cried Dichu, turning to his followers, "these men are friends and not enemies."

As friends, then, Dichu led them to his house and made them welcome. The fearless bravery of Patrick and his strong kind face had won the chieftain's heart, and he prepared to entertain him royally. But Patrick could neither rest nor eat until his message was delivered, and as Dichu listened to his burning words, they seemed to seize him with a strange power and made him long to hear more. Gladly would he have kept Patrick with him, but there was much work to be done, and the bishop wished first of all to seek out his old master Michu, and pay the money due to him as the price of the runaway slave.

How well he knew every step of the way to the old farm! It seemed as if he must be walking in a dream, that he must be still the barefooted, hungry, ill-clad boy of long ago. There were the woods through which he had so often driven his pigs, the banks where he had found the first spring flowers, the rocks which had so often sheltered him, the little green friendly shamrock which he had loved so dearly. Up the steep hillside he climbed, and at the top he paused and knelt in prayer, remembering the vision he had seen there and the message of the angel. Then, rising up, he looked eagerly towards the spot where his master's farm nestled in the hollow beneath.

Alas! he had come too late; nothing but a thin grey curl of smoke marked the place where the smouldering ashes of the farm lay, and, saddest of all, his master too had perished in the fire.

So there was naught to do but turn back and carry the message to others. But Patrick's heart was sad for his old master.

The glad season of Easter was close at hand, but it held no meaning for the people of this dark land. True, they had their own religion, a strange worship of the sun, and their priests, who were called Druids, were said to possess magical powers and great wisdom. They had great festivals too in which all the people joined, and one of these was just about to be held at Tara. Here the Druids were all assembled to do honour to the sun, which was becoming powerful enough to put winter to flight and warm the spring buds into summer blossoms. For some days before the feast, every fire was put out, and not a light was allowed to be kindled, on pain of death, until the great festal light should be lighted on the Hill of Tara.

Now Patrick was brave as a lion, and his heart was set on delivering his message and spreading the True Light in this heathen darkness, so there was no room for fear. The gathering of the priests and the presence of the powerful King Laoghaire seemed to him a splendid opportunity of fighting the powers of evil.

Across hill and dale he travelled swiftly with his little band of followers until he reached the Hill of Slane, close to Tara. There, on Easter Eve, when the land was wrapt in darkness, when not the faintest glimmer of a light could be seen in the solemn blackness that brooded over Tara's Hill, he lit his Easter fire and watched the tongues of flame as they shot up and lighted the whole country round.

The King and his councillors the Druids came hastily together in anger and astonishment when they saw the glowing light.

"Who has dared to do this thing?" asked the King in a fury.

"It is none of our people," said the priest: "it is the challenge of an enemy."

The wise men were troubled and talked together in half-fearful tones. There was an ancient prophecy which rung in their ears, and made them wonder if the man they had seen wending his way at the head of his little company that day to the Hill of Slane was possessed of some magic power.

Slowly one of the Druids chanted the verse, while the others listened sullenly.

> "He comes, he comes with shaven crown,
>   from off the storm-tossed sea,
> His garment piercèd at the neck,
>   with crook-like staff comes he.
> Far in his house, at its east end,
>   his cups and patins lie.
> His people answer to his voice:
>   Amen, Amen, they cry. Amen, Amen."

"Whoe'er he be, he shall not come to challenge our power," quoth the King. "We will go forth and punish this bold stranger."

Down the dark silent hillside the King and his councillors rode furiously, and never stopped until they reached the Hill of Slane. But there the Druids called a halt.

"Let a messenger be sent to fetch forth the man," they said; "we will not venture within the line of his magic fire."

"We will receive him here," said the King, "and let no man rise when he approaches lest he should think that in any way we seek to honour him."

So the men sat down silently to wait until the messenger should return, and ere long Patrick was seen to come swiftly down the hill towards them. That was the man, there was no doubt of it. As he came nearer they could see the shaven crown, the robe pierced at the neck, and in his hand the crook-like staff, while from the hill-top could be heard the music of the Easter hymn and the chanting of the loud "Amen."

The company sat silent and unmoved as Patrick approached. Only one little lad, watching with intent eyes the face of the stranger, rose to his feet in reverent greeting, forgetting the King's command.

A gentle look came into Patrick's eyes as he noticed the eager greeting and, raising his hand, he blessed the little lad.

"Who art thou, and what is thy errand here?" thundered the King.

"I am a torchbearer," answered Patrick. "I bring the True Light to lighten this dark land, to spread around peace and goodwill. All I ask is that thou wilt hear my message."

SAINT PATRICK

Alone and unarmed but quite fearless, Patrick stood up before the angry men next day, and spoke such words as they had never heard before. It was a new and wonderful teaching, and many of the wise men and nobles listened eagerly; and when he was done they came and asked to be baptized and enrolled under the banner of Patrick's God.

That was a glad Eastertide for the bishop, and as time went on the light spread far and wide. Many there were who shut their eyes and loved the darkness rather than the light, but Patrick was wise in his dealings with them all. He was never harsh or scornful of their beliefs, but always tried to lead them through what was good and beautiful in their own religion, using old customs and feasts to do honour to Christ, giving them a new meaning that linked them to His service.

Then, too, he wisely tried to win over the chief men of the land to become Christians, knowing that their followers would the more readily follow their masters. Young boys were also his special care, remembering as he always did his bitter years of lonely slavery, and these lads were to him as sons. The boy he had blessed on that Easter Eve on the hillside of Slane was now one of his followers, and years afterwards we hear of him as Bishop of Slane. It was one of these lads whom Patrick loved so well, whose bravery and loyal devotion once saved the good bishop's life.

Coming one day to the spot where a great stone marked the place of the Druids' worship, Patrick overthrew the stone that he might set up an altar instead. This was considered a terrible insult, and one of the heathen chiefs vowed that, come what might, he would kill Patrick wherever he found him.

Now the lad who drove Patrick's chariot heard this threat, and accordingly guarded his master with increased watchfulness. At last, however, his enemy's opportunity came, for Patrick's journeying took him past the chief's abode. The boy Oran knew that his master had no fear and would never turn aside to escape danger, so, as they neared the place, he thought of a plan to save him.

"I grow so weary with this long day of driving, my master," he said. "My hands can scarce hold the reins. If thou wouldst but drive for a space and let me rest, all would be well."

"Thou shouldst have asked sooner, my son," said the bishop kindly. "I am but a hard master to overtask thy strength."

So saying, Patrick changed seats, and gathering up the reins, drove on, while the boy sat behind in his master's seat, and prayed that the gathering darkness might close in swiftly, so that no one could mark the change.

Very soon they reached the outskirts of a dense wood, and from the sheltering trees a dark figure sprang out. The frightened horse reared for a moment, there was a singing sound of some weapon whizzing through the air, and when Patrick turned to see what it meant, the boy lay dead with a javelin in his heart—the murderer's weapon, which had been meant for the master. Well might Patrick, as he knelt there in his bitter grief, bear in his heart the echo of his Master's words, "Greater love hath no man than this, that a man lay down his life for his friends."

Journeying on from place to place teaching the people, Patrick came at one time to Cruachan, and there, by the well of Clebach, he stopped to rest in the early morning with his little band of followers. Very earnestly they talked together in the dim morning light, and they had no eyes to notice the glorious golden banners flung out in the east to herald the rising sun, nor did they notice two white-clad figures that came stealing up towards the well where they sat.

When the day is just awakening, and the stillness and mystery of the night still lies hid in sleepy hollows and shadowy woods, there is a magic spell upon the earth. It is the same old world, and yet all is fresh, all is good and beautiful. Fear is not yet awake. Wild creatures are tame and friendly. Who would hurt them in this magic hour? Every flower holds its drop of dew close at its heart; there will be time enough to open later on when the sunbeams steal in and drink the crystal drops. Some there are who call this time "God's hour," and say the strange hush and peacefulness are there because the good God walks through His world at dawn.

It was at this hour that King Laoghaire's two daughters, Ethne and Fedelin, stole up the hillside to bathe in the clear waters of the Clebach spring. Hand in hand they climbed, glancing half fearfully at the hollows where the shadows still lingered, and speaking in whispers lest they should frighten the fairies that had been dancing all night on the hillside.

Suddenly, when they came in sight of the well, they stopped in amazement and half in fear. Had they caught the fairies at last, or were these spirits, these quiet solemn men seated there like a circle of grey ghosts?

Slowly Ethne the Fair went forward and spoke to the spirit who seemed to be king among the rest.

"Whence do you come?" she asked, "and what is your name?"

Fedelin the Ruddy then drew near to hear the answer. She was no longer afraid when she saw how kindly was the look in the stranger's eyes.

"Nay," answered Patrick, "it matters little who I am and whence I came, for I must soon pass away. Better it were to seek to know the God whom I serve, for He liveth for ever."

"Who is your God?" asked Ethne, "and where is He? Is He in heaven or in earth, in the sea or in mountains?"

"How can we know Him?" asked Fedelin. "Where is He to be found?"

"My God is the God of all men, and He is everywhere," answered Patrick. Then, pointing to the rosy east, the mist-wrapt mountains and homely meadowland, he told them how God had made the world and all that is in it, how He loved it, and had sent His son, born of a pure virgin, to redeem it.

"He is the King of Heaven and Earth," said Patrick, "and it is meet that ye, the daughters of an earthly king, should also be the children of the heavenly King."

It was a wonderful story, and the two maidens listened with breathless attention. "Teach us most diligently how we may believe in the heavenly King," they said. "Show us how we may see Him face to face, and whatsoever thou shalt say unto us, we will do."

The clear water of the fountain was close at hand, and Patrick led the two fair princesses to the brink and there baptized them in the name of Christ.

"Yet can ye not see the King face to face," he said, "until ye sleep in death and your souls shall wing their way up to His starry chamber."

The maidens earnestly prayed that they might not have long to wait, and the old story tells us that then they "received the Eucharist of God, and they slept in death." Like two fair flowers just opening their petals in the dawning light, the Master's hand gathered them before the heat and dust of the working day had time to wither their freshness or soil their spotless purity.

Many there were besides these gentle maidens who learned to believe in Patrick's God. His teaching came like a trumpet-call to the strong men and lawless chieftains who ruled the land. They were brave and fearless warriors these heathen chiefs, men who met pain and suffering with unflinching courage and scorned to show their hurt; men after Patrick's own heart, fit soldiers to serve his King. There was one, Aengus by name, King of Munster, who gladly obeyed the call and welcomed Patrick to his palace, asking that he might be baptized and received as God's servant. The water was brought and Patrick, leaning on his crozier, did not notice that the sharp point was resting on the foot of Aengus. Deeper and deeper the point pierced the bare foot as Patrick went through the service, but not a sign did the brave man make. This, he thought, must be part of his baptism, and he was ready, nay, eager to endure hardness as a good soldier of Jesus Christ.

Not until Patrick tried to lift his staff did he perceive what he had done, and then, in spite of his sorrow, the sight of that pierced foot made him thank God in his heart for a brave man's endurance.

It was the custom of many of these chieftains when they became Christians, to give Patrick a piece of land on which to build a church, so ere long churches and monasteries were built wherever Patrick journeyed, and there he left teachers to carry on his work. All who loved learning found their way to these monasteries, and among them were many of the Druids, who were the poets and musicians of that time. They tuned their harps now in God's service, and so beautiful was the music they made that it is said "the angels of heaven stooped down to listen," and the harp became the badge of Christian Ireland.

SAINT PATRICK

As a rule Patrick was allowed to choose which piece of land he wanted, but when he came to Armagh, the chieftain, whose name was Daire, would only allow him to have a piece of low-lying meadowland, and refused to give him the good place on the hillside which Patrick had wanted. Then, perhaps feeling a little ashamed of himself, he thought that he would make it up to the good bishop by presenting him with a splendid present. This was a wonderful brass cauldron which had been brought from over the sea, and there was no other like it in the land. So Daire came to where Patrick was and presented the cauldron.

"This cauldron is thine," said Daire. "Gratzacham" (I thank thee), answered the saint. That was all, and Daire went home, becoming more and more angry as he went.

"The man is a fool," he said; "he can say nothing for a wonderful cauldron of three firkins except Gratzacham."

Then, turning to his slaves, he added: "Go and bring us back our cauldron."

So back they went and said to Patrick, "We must take away the cauldron." And all that Patrick said was, "Gratzacham, take it."

Now, when they returned to Daire, carrying the cauldron, he asked them, "What said the Christian when ye took away the cauldron?"

"He said Gratzacham again," answered the slaves.

"He saith the same when I give as when I take away," said Daire. "He is a man not easily moved, and he shall have his cauldron back."

And not only was the cauldron returned, but the chieftain himself came to Patrick and told him he should have the piece of land which he desired. Together they went to climb the hill, and when they came to the place they found there a roe lying with her fawn. The men ran forward and would have killed the fawn, but Patrick was quicker than they, and he lifted the little creature gently in his arms and carried it to another place of safety. The roe seemed to know he was a friend, and trotted happily by his side until he stooped down and gave her back her fawn once more. Some say that the altar of the great cathedral of Armagh covers the spot where once on the grassy hillside the fawn found a shelter in the arms of Saint Patrick.

The years went by, and each day was filled by Patrick with service for his Master, until the useful life drew to a close. Then, in the spring of the Year, when the March winds were blowing, when the shamrocks he loved were decking the land in dainty green, came the King's command, "Come up higher." It was but a gentle call, for he had dwelt so close to the Master that it was only a step from the Seen to the Unseen, and he needed no loud summons, for his feet were on the threshold of home.

"Christ with me, Christ before me,
Christ behind me, Christ within me,
Christ beneath me, Christ above me,

> Christ at my right, Christ at my left,
> Christ in the fort,
> Christ in the chariot-seat,
> Christ in the ship."

So runs part of the beautiful old hymn of Saint Patrick, and we do not wonder that he who was so truly a follower of Christ came to be called a saint.

A helpless captive, a hard-worked slave, a lonely swineherd! Who would have dreamed that to him would have belonged the honour of leading into freedom and light the land of his captivity? Who would have thought that the lowly slave would be the torchbearer of the King, the patron saint of the green isle of Erin?

SAINT DAVID

THERE is an old legend which tells us that the good Saint Patrick, before he returned to the Green Island where he had been a slave, stayed for a while in Wales and thought to make his home there. He loved its wild mountains and deep glens dearly, its dancing streams and purple cliffs rising so straight from the edge of the blue sea. There was much work there, too, waiting to be done, and he thought that he was the man to do it. But one evening, as he sat at sundown upon the steep rock of Cam Ilidi, a messenger of God was sent in a vision to change his purpose. It was a fitting time and place for a heavenly vision. Below him the heathery moors sloped down to the edge of the sea, whose blue waters stretched out their shining glory of sapphire and gold in the sunset glow, and above in the sky the clouds were flinging wide their banners of rose and crimson. So full was the very air of wondrous light and colour that the angel who stood beside him seemed but a part of the shining glory.

"Dost thou see," said the angel, "beyond yon golden sea, a dim blue line beneath the sunset edge? That is the land where thou shalt dwell and wage thy warfare for God, the land from whence thou shalt enter into thy rest. This country is not for thee, but is reserved for one who shall be born thirty years hence." So it was that Saint Patrick went to Ireland, while Wales waited for the saint whom God should send.

Full thirty years then passed away before Saint David, patron saint of Wales, was born. His father, it is said, was kin to King Arthur, and his mother was a poor Irish nun. Leaving her monastery, the gentle nun went to live in a cottage at the edge of the cliffs, above a little bay which is still called by her name. Here, while the wild winds dashed the spray far up the cliffs and shrieked like demons around the little cottage, her baby was born.

Perhaps the favourite name of all others in Wales has ever been David or Dewi. Sometimes it is spelt Dafyd, and the old nickname "Taffy" may have been the way which English tongues pronounced it. It was this name of David which they gave to the baby born in the wind-swept cottage that stormy night, little guessing that it was to be the name of the patron saint of Wales.

Like other children wild and free, he grew up strong and hardy; learned to climb the rocks like a young goat and to live his life out of doors, the sky above for his roof and the thymy grass for his carpet. But that was when he was but a little boy. Growing older, there were lessons to be learned and duties to be done, and so young David was sent to be tamed and taught at the monastery school.

Paulinus, his master, loved the boy, and found him quick to learn and easy to teach. In the old stories of Saint David's life there is not much told of his childhood, but it is said that "David grew up full of grace and lovely to be looked at. And he learned at school the psalms, lessons of the whole year, mass and communion; and there his fellow disciples saw a dove with a golden beak playing about his lips, and singing the hymns of God."

Pure lips from which no ugly word ever fell, kindly speech that turned quarrels into friendliness, straightforward truth and honour, that was what his companions noted when they watched young David, and this was why perhaps they spoke of the dove with golden beak that played about his lips.

One other thing the old story tells about the boy. Paulinus the master suffered once from a dreadful pain in his eyes. For a time he could see nothing and feel nothing but his misery, and he did not know when David came and stood beside him in pitying silence. But presently he felt cool hands laid on his aching eyes, a tender touch that gently stroked the hot suffering eyelids until in some miraculous fashion it charmed the pain away.

As the Master of old in Galilee brought peace and healing by the touch of His kind hand, it is not strange that those who walk closest in His footprints should have learned from Him the virtue that lies in a tender loving touch.

SAINT DAVID

PURE LIPS FROM WHICH NO UGLY WORD EVER FELL

There were rough times to be faced when David grew to manhood and became the head of his monastery. Not only was the land continually plundered by foreign foes, but there were still many bards and chieftains who hated Christianity and looked upon David as their foe. The love of music and poetry was as strong in the land as the love of the sword, and these bards were the teachers of the people, poets who sang of the great deeds of heroes, and told in flowing verse of their victories and defeats. Thus it was a great matter to win these bards to the service of Christ, and David counted it a great victory when they listened to his teaching and were willing to enter Christ's service. The monasteries welcomed them eagerly, knowing that the music of their harps lifted men's souls to heaven.

So the banner of Christ floated more and more triumphantly over the land, and one by one the monasteries were founded by David, and filled with men eager to take service under that banner. It was no easy life that tempted men to become monks in those days. Saint David's rule was so strict that only those who were willing to endure hardness could have found pleasure in living as they did. Clothes rough and coarse, made from the skins of animals, food of the simplest, work of some sort from morning till night, this was what Saint David's followers willingly endured. Every moment of the day had its duties, either prayer or hard work in the fields. Instead of oxen or horses, the monks themselves were harnessed to the plough, and patiently plodded through the work given to them to do.

But through it all the love of beauty and music and poetry was never crushed out, but rather grew stronger in these simple monks. One thing they loved above all, and that was to make copies of the Holy Book, and each one strove to make his copy as fair and exquisite as skill could achieve. So much did they love this work that a special rule was obliged to be made, which ordered that when the church bell rang the brothers were to stop work at once, the sentence be left unfinished, and even the word left half written. Instant obedience was one of the first things David's monks learned, and it taught them how to conquer the world.

Upon the same rock of Saint Patrick's vision David built his own beloved monastery, and there, in sight of the sea he loved and those purple hills of glory, he too received the heavenly messenger and heard the summons, "Friend, come up higher."

SAINT MOLIOS

IN the days of long ago, an old legend tells us, there lived a holy man whose heart was so filled with tender compassion for others that it even grieved him to think that there lay in the church-yard poor forgotten dead people for whom no one cared.

So, when the busy work of the day was done, this holy man made his way to the churchyard, and knelt and prayed there beside the lonely graves. He prayed so earnestly that he never noticed that the sun had set and the twilight was creeping on, and he never saw the silver moon as it rose over the hill. Hour after hour passed, and all the village lights were out, but still the saint knelt on in the churchyard. And then it was that the angels came.

They came in solemn procession, robed in white, with silver censers in their hands, but there was no great glory or heavenly light around them, and the saint thought they were a company of priests passing through the churchyard. Only their garments were whiter than any earthly robes, and the perfume that rose from the silver censers was sweeter than anything on earth.

SAINT MOLIOS

Here and there among the grass-grown mounds the procession stayed, and the censers were swung as if before the shrine of a saint. They were but poor neglected graves by which the white-robed angels stopped, some without even a name to mark them, and some among the nettles, where the grass grew so high and rank that there was scarcely a trace to show a grave was there at all. But even there the silver censers were swung on high, and the incense, sweet as the breath of flowers, floated up to heaven.

Each night the holy man returned to pray in the quiet churchyard, and each night the white-robed figures came and went, and the saint longed to ask them what they did. At last, taking courage, he stopped them and put his question. But even as he spoke he knew that these were no earthly priests but a company of angels.

"We are God's messengers," answered one of the white-robed throng, "sent by Him to do honour to His saints whose bodies lie forgotten here. Even their dust is dear to Him, and although the world has forgotten them, He marks their hallowed graves. Each night He sends us to His garden, where His seeds are sown which shall one day, like the flowers, blossom into a more glorious body."

It is a beautiful thought which this old legend teaches us—the thought that even the dust of God's saints is precious in His sight. It comes as a comforting message when we find how quickly the busy world forgets even the names of those saints to whom it owes so much; when the visions which have kept the world in touch with heaven have been forgotten and faith grows dim.

Among the many half-forgotten churchyards there is one in the little clachan of Shiskine among the Arran hills, where perhaps there is many a humble mound over which the angels swing their silver censers; and we know at least one saint by name whose dust lies there. A flat grey stone covers the grave, and on it is cut the name of Saint Molios and his story still lingers in the memory of the old folk in the country round, although to the young ones he is little more than a name.

But when winter comes, and the evenings are dark and long, the children often ask for a story, and are content then to listen to the tale of Saint Molios. The old grandmother in her white mutch sits in the armchair close to the fire, while the children gather round on their little stools. The sweet scent of peat smoke fills the kitchen and wraps everything in a blue haze, so that the oil-lamp which hangs from the rafters above scarcely lifts the shadows from the dark corners where cupboard-beds can dimly be seen.

"Och ay," says the grandmother, a smile on her sweet old face as her mind goes back to the past, "He was a good man was he they ca' Saint Molaise. Folk say he lived a terrible strict life over yonder in the Holy Isle, close to Lamlash. His house was a wee bit cave, high up among the rocks, and a' he had for a bed was a shelf cut oot o' the side o' the rock, scarcely wide eneuch to turn in. He had a bath too, doon by the sea, for he was aye fond o' the water, and summer and winter he would go in to wash."

Here for a moment her eye rested upon a little grimy upturned face, which blushed and hid itself against her petticoat.

"He knew it was a good thing to keep the body clean as well as the soul. All alone he lived with no a body to help him, and all the time he had for idleness he was praying and praising God. 'Twas him that brocht the Gospel to the Arran folk, and aften he would cross the hills and come awa' doon to the clachan here, and teach and preach the Word o' God.

"If ony o' the folk were in trouble and needed a friend, it was to Molaise they turned, and he was aye ready to help, not only with the words o' comfort, but with kind acts as well. The poor loved his very name, and the bairns would rin by his side haudin' on to his hand: they likit fine to look up and see the smile on his face. Awa' doon by his cave the sea-birds would come fleein' roond as if they too had come to listen to the good words o' the saint, and the wild deer in the bracken would just gie him a friendly look and go on chumping away at the grass as he passed. They werena feart for him, for a' beasts ken well eneuch that when a man loves God he loves God's craturs too.

"There were few graveyards in Arran in those days, and they carried most o' the dead to the wee kirkyard here; and so, when the good man died, they brocht his body across the island and laid him there at the foot o' the hills, where the burn is aye singing; where the grey stones stand so straight and solemn, pointing up the glen.

"They made a picter of Saint Molaise cut oot o' the stone, and put it there to show where he was laid. And there it lay, winter and summer, for hundreds and hundreds o' years, so they say. And when I was a bairn we had no gran' picter books like what ye have now. The only picter we had was the old stone of Molaise, and we a' loved it and thocht it awfu' bonnie. And when we had a holiday frae the schule it was always there we went, to the wee kirkyard to see the picter on Molaise's stone.

"Whenever a baby was born in the clachan, its mother would go and pit a silver saxpence on the old stone, a kind o' thanksgiving they ca'ed it. But the saxpence never bade there for long, and we bairns aye thocht it was ta'en awa' by Sandy the herd. He was a puir body was Sandy, no quite like ither folk, and he was aye sae joyful when he heard o' a birth in the clachan. There's a queer kind o' crack across the old stone just above where the saint's knees would come, and my mither would sometimes be telling us the tale of how that happened. It was one day, she said, when they would be bringing an old man from the north end o' the island to be buried at Shiskine. There were no roads then where they could drive a cart, so they had to carry the chest on long spakes; and one o' the young men when he got to the kirkyard would be very tired and kind o' impatient, for it had been a heavy job. So he flung down the spake while he would be swearing, and it fell across the saint's stone and crackit it clean across by the knees. An' that very night, when the young man was finding his way home above the cliffs o' Drumadoon, he slippit and fell, and they found him next morning with baith his legs broken clean across, in the very same place where he had cracked Molaise's stone. Mind I'm no sayin' that was the reason he slippit and hurt himself. Maybe it was, maybe it wasna. But ye can see the crack across the old stone to this day.

"Och ay, but ye wunna find the stone in the old place now. They couldna let it bide in the place where it had always been, but they must take it up to be an ornament for the gran' new kirk, and poor Molaise's picter stands there now, and the grave has only a plain grey stone to mark it.

"Never a hand in the clachan could be bribed to lift that stone, and so they brocht men from the ither side o' the island and took it away in the mirk when no a body saw. Ay, but they say that after moving the saint's picter, one o' the men driving home in the cart met with a terrible accident, for the wheel came off the cart, and the man was coupit oot and was very near killed."

So runs the old woman's story, and if you wander up the glen by the side of the surging burn, past the little ruined church to the old churchyard, you will find among the long dank grass the tomb of Saint Molios. The purple heather grows close to the churchyard gate; the silent hills, like great watchers, keep guard over God's little garden there; and it seems a fitting place for the saint of Arran to take his rest "until the day break, and the shadows flee away."

SAINT BRIDGET

THE mist of long years enfolds the story of Bridget, the dearly loved saint of Ireland. Though we strive to see her clearly, the mist closes round and only lifts to show us, here and there, a flash of light upon her life, and while we gaze in wonder the light is gone.

But all the time, behind the mist, we feel there is a gracious presence, a white-robed maiden with a pure strong soul, who dwelt in the green isle of Erin; a gentle saint who dwells there still in the hearts of her people to bless and comfort them as of old. The mist of years cannot dim the eyes of those who love Saint Bridget's memory, nor can it bewilder their faithful hearts. Wise men may dispute the facts of her life, but to the poor, who love her, she is just their friend, the dear Saint Bridget whose touch made sick folk well, whose blessing increased the store of the poor, who helped sad weary mothers, and bent in loving tenderness over many a tiny cradle in those long ago days.

So now it comforts the mother's heart, when there are many little hungry mouths to fill, to remember how Saint Bridget's faith ever found a way to feed the poor and needy. When the cradle is made ready for the little one whom God will send, it is for Saint Bridget's blessing that the mother prays, counting it the greatest gift that God can give. She is such a homelike saint this Bridget of the fair green island, and she dwells so close to the heart of the people, that it is their common everyday life which holds the most loving memory of her helpful kindness.

In the first days of early spring her little flame-spiked flowers speak to them from the roadside, and bring her message of joy and hope, telling of the return of life, the swelling of green buds, the magic of the spring. We call her flower the common dandelion, but to Saint Bridget's friends it is "the little flame of God" or "the flower of Saint Bride." She herself has many names. Bride or Bridget, "Christ's Foster-Mother," Saint Bridget of the Mantle, the Pearl of Ireland.

Many stories and legends have grown up around the memory of Saint Bridget, but all agree in telling us that she was a little maiden of noble birth, and that her father, Dubtach, was of royal descent. We know too that she was born in the little village of Fochard in the north of Ireland, about the time when good Saint Patrick was beginning to teach the Irish people how to serve the Lord Christ.

Bridget was a strange thoughtful child, fond of learning, but clever with her hands as well as her head. In those days even noble maidens had plenty of hard work to do, and Bridget was never idle. In the early morning there were the cows to drive out to pasture, when the dew hung dainty jewels upon each blade of grass and turned the spiders' webs into a miracle of flimsy lace. The great mild-eyed cows had to be carefully herded as they wandered up the green hillside, for, should any stray too far afield, there was ever the chance of a lurking robber ready to seize his chance. Then, when the cows were safely driven home again, there was the milking to be done and the butter to be churned.

But in spite of all this work, Bridget found time for other things as well. There was always time to notice the hungry look in a beggar's face as she passed him on the road, time to stop and give him her share of milk and home-made bread, time to help any one in pain who chanced to come her way. The very touch of the child's kind, strong little hands seemed to give relief and many a poor sufferer blessed her as she passed, and talked of white-robed angels they had seen walking by her side, guiding and teaching her. And sure it was that in all that land there was no child with so kind a heart as little Bridget's, and no one with as fair a face.

Now the older Bridget grew the more and more beautiful she became, and her loveliness was good to look upon. She was as straight and fair as a young larch tree; her hair was yellow as the golden corn, and her eyes as deep and blue as the mountain lakes. Many noble lords sought to marry her, but Bridget loved none of them. There was but one Lord of her life, and she had made up her mind to serve Him.

SAINT BRIDGET OF THE MANTLE

"We will have no more of this," said her father angrily; "choose a prince of noble blood, and wed him as I bid thee."

"I have chosen the noblest Prince of all," said Bridget steadfastly, "and He is the Lord Christ."

"Thou shalt do as thou art bidden and marry the first man who asks thee," said her brothers, growing more and more angry.

But Bridget knew that God would help her, and prayed earnestly to Him. Then in His goodness God took away her beauty from her for a while, and men, seeing she was no longer fair to look upon, left her in peace.

At this time Bridget was but a young maiden of sixteen years, but old enough, she thought, to give up her life to the service of God. The good Bishop Maccail, to whom she went, was perplexed as he looked at the young maid and her companions. Did she know what God's service meant, he wondered? Was she ready to endure hardness instead of enjoying a soft life of pleasure and ease?

But even as he doubted, the legend says, he saw a strange and wonderful light begin to shine around the maiden's head, rising upwards in a column of flame, and growing brighter and brighter until it was lost in the glory of the shining sky.

"Truly this is a miracle," said the Bishop, shading his eyes, which were blinded by the dazzling light. "He who, each morning, sendeth His bright beams aslant the earth to wake our sleeping eyes, hath in like manner sent this wondrous light to clear my inward vision and show my doubting heart that the maiden is one whom God hath chosen to do His work."

Even then the careful Bishop sought to know more of Bridget's life ere he trusted the truth of the miracle. But there was nought to tell that was not good and beautiful. Out on the green hills, at work in the home, all her duties had been well and carefully performed. Happy, willing service had she given to all who needed her help, and there was but one fault to be found with her.

"She gives away everything that comes to her hand," said her parents. "No matter how little milk the cows are giving, the first beggar who asks for a drink has his cup filled. If there is but one loaf of bread in the house, it is given away. The poor have but to ask, and Bridget will give all that she can find."

"That is true," said Bridget gently, "but ye would not have me send them hungry away? Is it not Christ Himself we help when we help His poor?"

"Well, well, perhaps thou art right," answered her parents; "and this we must say, that in spite of all that is given away, we have never wanted aught ourselves, but rather our store has been increased."

Hearing all this, the Bishop hesitated no longer, but laid his hands in blessing upon Bridget's head, and consecrated both her and her companions to the service of God. And it is said that as she knelt before the altar, while the Bishop placed a white veil upon her head, she leaned her hand upon the altar step, and at her touch the dry wood became green and living once more, so pure and holy was the hand that touched it. At first there were but few maidens who joined themselves with Bridget in her work, but as time went on the little company grew larger and larger. Then Bridget determined to build their home beneath the shelter of an old oak tree which grew near her native village. It was from this oak tree that the convent was known in after years as "the cell of the oak" or Kil-dare. Here the poor and those in distress found their way from all parts, and never was any poor soul turned away without help from the good sisters and the tender-hearted Bridget. Here the sick were healed, the sorrowful comforted, and the hungry fed. Here the people learned to know the love of Christ through the tender compassion of His servant.

Far and near the fame of Bridget spread, not only in Ireland but over many lands, and the love of her became so deeply rooted in the hearts of the people, that even to-day her memory is like a green tree bearing living leaves of faith and affection.

There are so many wonderful stories clustering round the name of Saint Bridget that they almost make her seem a dim and shadowy person, but there is one thing that shines through even the wildest legend. The tender heart and the helping hand of good Saint Bridget are the keynote of all the wonders that have been woven around her name. We see her swift on all errands of mercy, eager to help the helpless, ready to aid all who were oppressed, and protecting all who were too weak to help themselves.

One story tells us of a poor wood-cutter who by mistake had slain a tame wolf, the King's favourite pet, and who for this was condemned to die. As soon as the news was brought to Saint Bridget, she lost not a moment, but set out in the old convent cart to plead with the King for his life. Perhaps her pleading might have been in vain had it not been that as she drove through the wood a wolf sprang out of the undergrowth and leapt into the car. Loving all animals, tame or wild, Saint Bridget nodded a welcome to her visitor and patted his head, and he, quite contentedly, crouched down at her feet, as tame as any dog.

Arrived at the palace, Saint Bridget demanded to see the King, and with the wolf meekly following, was led into his presence.

"I have brought thee another tame wolf," said Saint Bridget, "and bid thee pardon that poor soul, who did thee a mischief unknowingly."

So the matter was settled to every one's satisfaction. The King was delighted with his new pet, the poor man was pardoned, and Saint Bridget went home rejoicing.

Those sisters who dwelt in the Cell of the Oak seemed to be specially protected from all harm, and it is said that many a robber knew to his cost how useless it was to try and rob Saint Bridget.

SAINT BRIDGET

Once there came a band of thieves who, with great cunning, managed to drive off all the cows belonging to the convent, and in the twilight to escape unnoticed. So far all went well, and the robbers laughed to think how clever they had been. But when they reached the river which they were obliged to cross, they found the waters had risen so high that it was almost impossible to drive the cows across. Thinking to keep their clothes dry, they took them off and bound them in bundles to the horns of the cows, and then prepared to cross the ford. But Saint Bridget's wise cows knew a better way than that, and immediately there was a stampede, and they set off home at a gallop, and never stopped until they reached the convent stable. The thieves raced after them with all their might, but could not overtake them, and so, crestfallen and ashamed, they had at last to beg for pardon and pray that their clothes might be returned to them.

In those days there were many lepers in Ireland, and when there was no one else to help and pity them, the poor outcasts were always sure of a kindly welcome from the gracious lady of Kildare. One of the stories tells of a wretched leper who came to Saint Bridget, so poor and dirty and diseased that no one would come near him. But like our blessed Lord, Saint Bridget felt only compassion for him, and with her own hands washed his feet and bathed his poor aching head. Then, seeing that his clothes must be washed, she bade one of the sisters standing by to wrap her white mantle round the man until his own clothes should be ready. But the sister shuddered and turned away; she could not bear to think of her cloak being wrapped around the miserable leper. Quick to mark disobedience and unkindness, a stern look came into Saint Bridget's blue eyes as she put her own cloak over the shivering form.

"I leave thy punishment in God's hands," she said quietly; and even as she spoke, the sister was stricken with the terrible disease, and as the cloak touched the beggar, he was healed of his leprosy.

Tears of repentance streamed down the poor sister's face, and her punishment was more than tender-hearted Saint Bridget could bear to see. Together they prayed to God for pardon, and at Saint Bridget's touch the leprosy was healed.

So Saint Bridget lived her life of mercy and loving-kindness, and because the people loved and honoured her above all saints, they placed her in their hearts next to the Madonna herself, and, by some curious instinct of tender love and worship, there came to be woven about her a legend which has earned for her the titles of "Christ's Foster-Mother" and "Saint Bridget of the Mantle."

It was on that night, so the legend runs, when the Blessed Virgin came to Bethlehem, weary and travel-worn, and could find no room in the village inn, that Saint Bridget was sent by God to help and comfort her. In the quiet hours of the starry night, when on the distant hills the wondering shepherds heard the angels' song, Saint Bridget passed the stable door and paused, marvelling at the light that shone with such dazzling brilliance from within. Surely no stable lantern could shed such a glow as that which shone around the manger there. Softly Saint Bridget entered and found the fair young Mother bending over the tiny newborn Child, wrapping His tender little limbs about with swaddling bands.

There was no need to ask who He was. Bridget knew it was the King, and kneeling there, she worshipped too. Then very tenderly she led the young Mother to a soft bed of sweet bay and prayed her that she would rest awhile.

"Sweet Mary," she implored, "rest, and I meanwhile will watch and tend the Child." And Mary, looking into Bridget's kind blue eyes, and feeling the touch of her tender strong hands, trusted her with her Treasure, and bade her take the Child and watch Him until the morning should break.

So Bridget took off her soft mantle and wrapped the Baby in it, and, sitting there, rocked Him to sleep, crooning to Him all the sweetest baby songs she knew.

Perhaps it was Saint Bridget's tender love for little children, and her gentle care for all poor mothers, that helped to weave this curious legend, but there is a beautiful truth hidden deep in the heart of the strange story too. For did not Christ Himself say of all kind deeds done to the poor, "Inasmuch as ye have done it unto one of the least of these my brethren, ye have done it unto Me"; and again, "Whosoever shall do the will of My Father which is in heaven, the same is My brother and sister and mother."

So it is that Saint Bridget bears the name of Christ's foster-mother and is linked in this loving way with the Mother of our Lord. Year by year her memory lives on, and when February, the month of Saint Bride, comes round, when the bleating of the first lambs is heard on the hills, and the little flower of Saint Bridget lights up the wayside with its tiny yellow flame, the thought of good Saint Bridget, Christ's foster-mother, fills many a poor mother's heart with comfort. Did she not care for all young things and helpless weary souls? Did she not show how, by helping others, she helped the dear Lord Himself? Does she not still point out the way by which they too may find Him and live in the light of His love?

SAINT CUTHBERT

IN all the countryside there was no other boy so strong and fearless as Cuthbert, the shepherd lad who dwelt amongst the hills above the old town of Melrose.

It was in the time when life was hard and rough, and there were but few comforts or luxuries even in the houses of the rich. The children in those days early learned to brave many a danger and suffer many a hardship, and so they grew up sturdy and strong of limb, accustomed to an open-air life, little heeding the icy winds of winter or the snow-storms that swept their southern border-lands of Scotland.

But among all these hardy children of the hills there was none to compare with Cuthbert. In all their games of skill or strength he easily won the foremost place. Whether it was winter and they played at mimic warfare, with wonderful snow castles to be stormed and good round snowballs for their ammunition, or whether it was summer time and they ran and wrestled on the grassy slopes of the hillside, it was Cuthbert who led the attack on the victorious side, Cuthbert who was champion among the wrestlers and swiftest in the race. When others grew tired and cried for a truce, Cuthbert was still fresh and eager, ready to urge them on, for he never seemed to know what it meant to give in. And yet there were times when the boy stole away silently by himself to a lonely part of the hill that overlooked the little grey road beneath, and there sat as quiet and motionless as the rabbits that peeped out of their holes in the rocks beside him. So still did he sit that any one seeing him might have thought he was asleep, if they had not seen his keen bright eyes and guessed that he was as busy with his thoughts as he had been about his games.

But there was no one on the wild hillside to watch the silent boy; only his little furry friends the rabbits stole out and nibbled the grass about his feet, and the birds came hopping around him, knowing they had nought to fear from one who never harmed them, waiting for the meal which he always shared with these his friends. Sometimes impatient of his long long thoughts, they would come nearer and peck at his bare feet, and Cuthbert would raise himself and chide them for their greediness, as he spread the crumbs which he had saved for them.

It was the little grey road beneath on which his eyes were fixed, and his thoughts followed its windings until it reached the old abbey of Melrose, the home of the holy monks, the servants of God. Sometimes he would see two or three of the brothers in their homespun cloaks passing beneath, and would listen to the soft notes of the vesper hymn as it floated upwards, and the eager light in his eyes grew ever brighter as he watched and listened. He

SAINT CUTHBERT

IT WAS THE LITTLE GREY ROAD BENEATH
ON WHICH HIS EYES WERE FIXED

knew what these good monks did for the people around; how they protected the weak, helped the helpless, nursed the sick, and went about unarmed and fearless through all the dangers that beset their path. There was something about the look of their kind strong faces that fascinated the boy, and drew him to watch for their passing and to dream of their work and their courage. Then he would softly sing over the fragments of their hymns which his keen ear had caught, and the sound stirred something in his soul.

"Who knows; some day I too may become a servant of God," he would whisper to himself. And it was a wonderful thought to dream about.

Then came a day which Cuthbert never forgot. He was playing as usual with the other boys, who were leaping and wrestling, and in their wild spirits trying to twist themselves into every kind of curious shape. They were all laughing and shouting together, when a little boy, scarce more than a baby, ran up and pulled Cuthbert by his coat.

"Why dost thou play such foolish games?" asked the child gravely.

Cuthbert stood still and looked down with surprise into the child's solemn eyes.

"Little wise one," he answered with a laugh, pushing him aside, but with no rough touch, "wilt thou teach us thy games of wisdom instead?"

The child turned away and with a sob flung himself upon the ground, crying as if his heart would break. The children gathered round, fearing he was hurt, but no one could find out what it was that vexed him, until Cuthbert lifted him up and soothed him with kindly words.

"Has aught harmed thee?" asked Cuthbert.

"No, no," sobbed the child; "but how canst thou, Cuthbert, chosen by God to be His servant and bishop, play at foolish games with babes, when He has called thee to teach thy elders?"

What strange words were these? The other boys had little patience with the crying child, and roughly bade him go home. But in Cuthbert's ears the words rang with a solemn sound, and he stored them up in his mind to ponder upon their meaning. What had the child meant? Was it possible that some day the words would come true and he would indeed be chosen by God to enter His service?

There was so much to think about that the lonely hours on the hillside grew longer and longer, and he but rarely joined in the games now. Even at night he could not rest, thinking those long long thoughts. He knew that the holy monks spent many a night in prayer to God, and he learned to love the dark solemn stillness when he crept out on the bare hillside to say his prayers under the starlit sky.

It seemed to be a link between him and those servants of God, and he thought in his childish way that if the angels were there to carry the holy prayers up to God's throne, they might in passing take his little prayer as well, and in that goodly company God would accept the best that a child could offer, knowing it was the prayer of one who longed to serve Him too.

As Cuthbert grew older there was less time for dreaming or for play. The sheep that were entrusted to him needed constant watchful care, for it was no easy task to be a shepherd in those wild days. Many an enemy lurked on the hillside, ready to snatch away a lamb if the shepherd was not careful. Not only did wolves prowl hungrily around, but men, not too honest, were as ready as the wolves to rob the flock, and it behoved the shepherd to be ever watchful and wary.

At night-time the shepherd lads would gather their sheep together and spend the hours in company watching round the fire, which they piled high with dried heather and dead branches from the wood. It was no hardship to Cuthbert, for he loved the long quiet nights on the hillside, and often while the others slept he watched alone, using the time for prayer.

He had helped to make the watch-fire as usual one night and had seen to the safety of the sheep, and then, one by one, the shepherd lads had fallen asleep in the warmth of the glowing fire. There was no need to rouse them, for he could keep guard alone, and he stole away a little apart to spend the night in prayer, as was his custom.

It was a dark night; the sky was velvet black, without even a star to prick a point of light through its heavy blackness, and the reflection of the fire served only to make the darkness more dense on the lonely hillside. Cuthbert could scarcely see the outline of the sheep, huddled together for warmth, and in that great silence and solitude God seemed very near. Then, as he knelt in prayer, gazing upwards, a vision such as that which gladdened the eyes of the shepherds of Bethlehem burst upon his view. A great stream of dazzling light broke through the darkness, as if a window in heaven had been opened, and in that white shaft of light a company of angels swept down to earth. It was no birthday message which they brought this time, but their song of triumph told of a good life ended, the crowning of a victor in a well-fought fight, as they bore upward the soul of one whose warfare was accomplished and who was entering into the joy of his Lord.

A great awe and joy filled the soul of Cuthbert as he gazed. Long after the last gleam of heavenly light had vanished, the last echo of the angels' songs had ceased, he knelt on there. This then was the glorious end of those who entered the service of God. "Fight the good fight: lay hold on eternal life"; was that an echo of the angels' song, or how was it that he seemed to hear the words spoken clearly in his ears?

With a cry Cuthbert sprang to his feet and ran back to the fire where the sleeping shepherds lay.

"Wake up, wake up," he cried, shaking them by the shoulders as he spoke. "How can ye sleep when ye might have beheld the vision of God's angels?"

The startled lads jumped up, wondering at first whether it might be an alarm of wolves or robbers, but even they were awed when they caught sight of Cuthbert's face and saw the light that shone upon it. With breathless interest they listened to the tale he had to tell of the angels' visit and the soul they had carried up to God. What could it all mean? They wished that they too had spent the night in prayer, instead of sleeping there.

Early in the morning, as soon as it was light and he could leave the sheep, Cuthbert found his way to the nearest hamlet, and there he learned that Aiden, the holy Bishop of Lindisfarne, had died that night.

So it was the soul of the good Bishop whose glorious end, nay rather whose triumphant new beginning, had been heralded by the angel throng. Cuthbert was awed to think that his eyes had been permitted to gaze upon that wondrous vision, and he felt that it must surely be a sign that God had given ear to his prayers, and would accept him as His servant. It was a call to arms; there should be no delay. He was eager and ready to fight the good fight, to lay hold on eternal life.

Before very long all his plans were made. It was but a simple matter to follow the example of the disciples of old, to leave all and to follow the Master. Only the sheep were to be gathered into the fold and their charge given up; only the little hut on the hillside to be visited, and a farewell to be said to the old nurse who dwelt there. Cuthbert had lost both father and mother when he was eight years old, and the old woman had taken charge of him ever since. She was sorely grieved to part with the lad, but she saw that his purpose was strong and that nothing would shake it. With trembling hands she blessed him ere he left her, and bade him not forget the lonely little hut on the hillside and the old nurse who had cared for him.

So at last all was ready, and Cuthbert set off down the hillside and along the little grey road that led to the monastery of Melrose, beside the shining silver windings of the Tweed.

Snow lay on all the hills around, and the wintry wind wailed as it swept past the grey walls and through the bare branches of the trees that clustered round the abbey. So mournful and so wild was the sound that it might have been the spirit of evil wailing over the coming defeat in store for the powers of darkness, when the young soldier should arrive to enrol his name in the army of God's followers.

At the door of the monastery a group of monks were standing looking down the darkening road for the return of one of the brothers. The prior Boisil himself was among them, and was the first to catch sight of a figure coming towards them with a great swinging stride. "A stranger," said one of the brothers, trying to peer through the gathering gloom.

"It is no beggar," said another. "Methinks it is a young knight. His steps are eager and swift, and he hath strong young limbs."

The prior said naught, but he too eagerly watched the figure as it came nearer. A strange feeling of expectancy had seized him. Something was surely about to happen which he had half unconsciously long waited for. Then, as the boy drew near and lifted his eager questioning eyes to the prior's face, the good man's heart went out to him.

"Behold a servant of the Lord." Very solemnly the words rang out as Boisil stretched out both hands in welcome, and then laid them in blessing upon the young fair head that was bowed before him.

The greeting seemed strange to the brethren gathered around. Who was this boy? What did their prior mean? But stranger still did the greeting sound in the ears of Cuthbert himself, and he could scarcely believe that he heard aright. "A servant of God": did the holy man really mean to call him, the shepherd lad, by that great name?

"Father," he cried, almost bewildered, "wilt thou indeed teach me how I may become God's servant, for it is His service that I seek?"

The prior smiled kindly at the anxious face, and bade him enter the monastery in God's name.

"My son," he said, "there is much for thee to learn, much to suffer, much to overcome, but surely the victory shall be thine."

So Cuthbert entered the monastery and the gates were shut. The old life was left behind and the new life begun.

The prior himself taught the boy his new lessons, for his love for the lad grew stronger and deeper each day. Boisil felt sure there was a great future before the youth, and he often dreamed dreams of the greatness in store for him and the work that he should do for God in the world.

"Who knows," he would say, "what honour God hath in store for thee. If heaven sends dreams, then is thy future sure, for I have seen thee wearing the bishop's mitre and holding the pastoral staff."

As for Cuthbert himself, he was too busy to think much of dreams or make plans for the future. Just as he had played his boyish games with all his might, so now he threw his whole soul into the work of the monastery. Lessons, prayer, fast and vigil, all were diligently attended to, and it was pleasant to see his glad cheerfulness when he was set to labour with his hands. The harder the task the more he seemed to enjoy it, and he rejoiced in the strength of his body which made him able to undertake much service. Although he now lived in the sheltered convent of the valley, his thoughts would often fly back, like homing birds, to the green hillsides, the glens and rocky passes, back to the little lonely weather-beaten hut where the old nurse lived. He never could forget the people who lived up there among the hills—poor shepherds, work-worn women and little children. It was a hard life they lived, with never a soul to bring them a message of hope or good cheer. Little wonder that their ways were often crooked and evil, and the thought of God but a far-off, dim, half-forgotten dream. Little wonder that black magic and

OUR ISLAND SAINTS

witchcraft should still have power to enchain them in their ignorance and fearfulness.

The good prior often talked with the eager young brother about these wandering sheep, and when the time came he sent Cuthbert out with his blessing to work amongst the hills once more, to gather the flock into the true fold.

How well did Cuthbert know those steep mountain paths! With what a light heart did he find his way over the rough hillsides where no paths were, to reach some cluster of huts where a few poor families lived, or even a solitary dwelling where some poor soul needed his care. There was something about the young monk that won a welcome for him wherever he went. Perhaps it was because he was so sure that all would rejoice to hear the message he brought; perhaps it was because he looked for the best in every one and so they gave him of their best.

From place to place Cuthbert went, and it mattered not to him how rough was the road or how terrific the storms that swept over the border-land. The snow might lie deep upon the hills, and he might be forced to spend the whole day without food, but no difficulty ever turned him back or forced him to leave one but unvisited.

Far and near the people began to look anxiously for his coming, and to listen eagerly to his teaching. There was always much for him to do; many a tale of sin to listen to, many a sinner to be taught the way of repentance. There were children, too, to be baptized, and this was work which

Cuthbert always loved. They were the little lambs of the flock to be specially guarded from the Evil One, who was ever prowling around to snatch them from the fold. The hut where the old nurse lived was often visited, for Cuthbert never forgot his friends.

There were other friends too that Cuthbert remembered and loved. His "little sisters the birds" soon learned to know and trust him again, and the wild animals of the hills grew tame under his hand. It is said that on one of his journeys, as he went to celebrate Mass with a little boy as server, they had finished all their food and were obliged to go hungry. Just then an eagle hovered above their heads and dropped a fish which it had just caught. The little boy seized it gladly and would have promptly prepared it for their meal, but Cuthbert asked if he did not think the kind fisherman deserved his share. The boy looked at the eagle and then at the small fish; but he knew what the master meant, so the fish was cut in half and the eagle swooped down to secure its share of the dinner.

There is another story told of the kindness shown by his furry friends to Saint Cuthbert, and it is a story which many people have remembered even when the history of Saint Cuthbert's life has been wellnigh forgotten.

It was when Cuthbert went to visit the holy Abbess of Coldingham, that, as was his wont when night came on, he wandered out to say his prayers in silence and alone. Now one of the brothers had long been anxious to know how it was that Cuthbert spent the long hours of the night, and so he stole down to the seashore and hid among the rocks, watching to see what would happen.

It was a cold bleak night, and the sea lay black and sullen outside the line of breakers, but Cuthbert seemed to have no fear of cold or blackness. Reaching the edge of the waves, he waded in deeper and ever deeper until the water rose as high as his chest. Standing thus, he sang his hymn of praise to God, and the sound of the psalms rose triumphant, hour after hour, above the sob of the sea and the wail of the wintry wind. Not till the first faint gleam of dawn touched the east with rosy light did Cuthbert cease his vigil of prayer and praise. Then, numbed and half frozen, he waded out and stood upon the shelving beach once more, and from the sea there followed him two otters. The watcher among the rocks saw the two little animals rub themselves tenderly against the frozen feet, until their soft fur brought back some warmth and life to the ice-cold limbs; and when their work was done they stole quietly back into the water and were seen no more. It is this legend of the kindness of the otters which has never been forgotten whenever the name of Saint Cuthbert is mentioned.

For fourteen years Cuthbert remained at Melrose, and when the good Boisil died the brethren chose the favourite young monk as their prior. But it was not long before he left the abbey of Melrose and went to the monastery of Lindisfarne, on the wild bleak island known as Holy Island. Here for twelve years he did his work as thoroughly and bravely as he had done when he was a monk at Melrose, and within the monastery his gentleness and infinite patience, his kindliness and wise dealing, smoothed away every difficulty, and brought peace and happiness to all the community.

It was no easy life he led on that bleak, bare, wind-swept island of the North Sea, but still Cuthbert sought for something harder and more difficult to endure. He longed to follow the example of the hermit saints of old, and he made up his mind to seek some desert spot where he might live alone with God, far from the world with its love of ease and its deadly temptations.

From the monastery of Lindisfarne, Cuthbert had often gazed across to the little islands which in summer-time shone like jewels set in a silver sea, and in winter seemed like little grey lonely ghosts wrapped in their shroud of easterly *haar*, or lashed by the cruel north wind until only the white foam of the breakers marked the spot where they stood. It was whispered by the brethren that evil spirits had their haunt upon the wildest of those little islands, and it seemed a fit place for the powers of darkness to work their will. There was not a tree and scarcely a plant upon the little island of Farne, for the bitter winds blew the salt spray in from every side, and only the wild sea-birds, gulls, kittiwakes, puffins, and eider-ducks, found shelter among the rocks to build their nests.

It seemed exactly the spot that Cuthbert sought for his retreat, and he only smiled when the brethren sought to dissuade him, and talked of the dangers that awaited any one who dared to land upon that island.

"Have we not ourselves heard the demon shrieks and their wild wicked laughter on stormy nights?" said one brother solemnly.

"Ay, and have we not seen the glitter of the demon lights set there to lure poor fishermen to their destruction?" said another.

"The greater need, then, that I should go," said Cuthbert. "Christ's soldier is the fittest champion to fight the powers of darkness."

So Christ's soldier went out to seek a home on the desolate island, and all alone there he set to work to found a little kingdom of his own. Whether the demons fled at the approach of the holy man, or whether they fought for their kingdom and were cast out by the might of Saint Cuthbert, or whether he found only the shrieking wind and wail of the wild birds instead of the howls of a demon crew, we know not. But certain it is that when at last some of the brothers ventured over, half timidly, to see how their prior fared, they found only Cuthbert and the wild birds there in peaceful solitude.

The hut which he had built for himself against the rocks was almost like a sea-bird's nest, for it was hollowed out deep within, and its walls were of rough stones and turf, its roof of poles and dried grass. It must have been a work of great labour to build that wall, and some of the stones were so large that it seemed as if it would have needed three men to move them.

"He could not have done it by himself," whispered the brethren; "it is God's angels who have helped him." And when, too, they found a spring of clear water gushing from the rock close to the little oratory, they said in their hearts, "He who turneth the stony rock into pools of water, hath here again shown His care for His servant."

At first it was needful that food should be brought to Cuthbert on the desolate island, but he was very anxious to provide for himself, for he always loved to work with his hands. The first crop of corn which he sowed came to nought, but the next thing he tried was barley, and that grew and flourished, and Cuthbert was content to think that now no longer was he dependent on others for his food. Yet it was but a scanty supply of grain that he had, and it was not without reason that the people whispered that the angels must bring food to the holy man, for he never seemed to lack the daily bread.

The wild birds that built their nests in the island of Farne soon grew accustomed to their new companion, and ceased to rise in white clouds when he came near. Of all the birds the eider-ducks were his special favourites and his special friends, and even to this day they are known by the name of Saint Cuthbert's ducks. So friendly did they become that, when the sunny month of June smiled on the little island and the mother duck was sitting upon her nest, she would allow Saint Cuthbert to come near and gently stroke her, and even let him peep inside at the hidden treasure—the five pale olive-coloured eggs that lay so snugly at the bottom of the nest.

For eight years Cuthbert lived his life of prayer and self-denial in the little home he had made for himself, but at the end of that time God had other work for him to do. In the world of strife and human passions the Church had need of a strong arm and a pure heart, and it was decided that the hermit of Farne Island should be called forth and made a bishop.

A company of men landed on the island and brought the message to the lonely man in his little oratory, but Cuthbert would not listen to their pleading. The honour was too great for him, he said, and he prayed them to leave him to his prayers. Then it was that the King himself, with the bishops and great men of the kingdom, came in a wondrous procession and besought Cuthbert to come out and do battle for God in the Church. Cuthbert saw then that it was the will of God, and very sorrowfully he yielded. It was with a sad heart that he left his home among the wild birds and prepared to take his place in the world again as Bishop of Lindisfarne. The dreams of Boisil, the good prior of Melrose, had indeed come true. The shepherd lad of the hills, the monk of Melrose, the prior of Lindisfarne, the hermit of Farne, now held the pastoral staff and wore the mitre of a bishop.

SAINT CUTHBERT

It was no mere sign of office that Cuthbert held in his hand the pastoral staff. He was indeed a shepherd and bishop of men's souls, and he guarded and tended his flock as carefully as in the old days he had tended the sheep upon the hills. Once again he trod the rough hilly paths and brought comfort and help to those who were afar off, and lit the lamp of faith that had grown dim. Sometimes, in the wild waste districts where there was no church and but few huts, the people would build a shelter for him with the boughs of trees, and there, in Nature's green cathedral, they would gather the children together for confirmation. Surely none of the little ones ever forgot that moment when they knelt before the good Bishop and felt the touch of his hand upon their bowed heads. The pale thin face was worn with suffering and hardship now, but the old sweet smile still drew all men's hearts out to him, and the love that shone in his eyes seemed more of heaven than of earth. He had always loved the lambs of the flock, and each little fair head upon which he laid his hand had a special place in his heart, as he gathered them into the fold of the Good Shepherd.

But it was not only the souls of his people for which Cuthbert cared, but for their bodies as well. Many an illness did he cure: many a stricken man owed his life to the Bishop's care. It seemed as if his very presence put fresh courage and strength into those who were thought to be dying, so that the touch of his hand led them back from the very gates of death. God had indeed given His servant special powers of healing, and who shall measure the power of a good man's prayers?

Once, in a far-off hamlet which had been visited by a deadly sickness, Cuthbert had gone from hut to hut, visiting and cheering each one of his people, leaving behind him courage and returning health. He was very weary and worn out, for the work had been heavy, but before leaving, he turned to a priest who was with him and said, "Is there still any one sick in this place whom I can bless before I depart?"

"There is still one poor woman over yonder," answered the priest. "One of her sons is already dead and the other is dying even now."

A few swift strides and the Bishop was by the side of the stricken mother. No thought had he of the danger of catching the terrible disease. His strong loving hands gently drew the dying child from her arms, and, holding the little one close to his heart, he knelt and prayed that God would spare the little life. Even as he prayed the child's breathing grew easier, and the cold cheek grew flushed and warm, and when he placed him again in his mother's arms it was a living child she held and not a dying one now.

But Cuthbert's strength was waning fast, and the old splendid health and strength were gone. He knew his work was drawing to a close and the days of his usefulness were over, and with the knowledge came a great longing to creep away to the little sea-girt island, and spend the last few months alone with God.

It was with heavy hearts that the brothers watched the little boat made ready which was to carry their beloved Bishop away from their care.

"Tell us, Reverend Bishop, when may we hope for thy return?" cried one.

"When you shall bring my body back," was the calm answer. Then they knew that this was their last farewell, and they knelt in silence to receive his blessing.

The end was not far off. A few short weeks amongst the happy birds; a worn weary body laying itself down to rest before the altar in the little oratory; a glad soul winging its triumphant flight back to God, and Saint Cuthbert's earthly life was over.

The end? Nay, there is no ending to the lives of God's saints, for they come down to us through the ages, a golden inheritance which can never die; stars in the dark night shining steadily on, with a light "which shineth more and more unto the perfect Day."

SAINT EDWARD THE CONFESSOR

King Edward of England, the last of the Saxon kings, sat in his chamber deep in thought and troubled beyond all measure. It was but a short while ago that he had been living in exile at the Norman Court, with little hope of returning to his native land, and now kind fortune had not only called him home but set him there as King upon the throne. One would have thought he had been granted more than his heart's desire and should have been content, but there were troubled lines on the King's forehead as he sat and thought of those days of exile.

Amidst all the gaiety and wild revels of the Norman Court, the exiled prince had seemed to live in a world apart from the pleasure-loving courtiers, with whom he had but little in common. He was a strange, dreamy boy, and even his appearance had something dreamlike about it. His soft shining hair was almost milky white in its fairness, and the rose pink of his cheeks made that curious whiteness seem truly dazzling by contrast. He had delicate hands, with long, thin, transparent fingers, and these hands, it was whispered, held a magic in their touch and could stroke away pain and charm away sickness.

While others talked of warlike deeds and boasted of wild adventures, he dreamed his dreams of the saints of old and the good fight which they had fought. Of all those saints the one he loved the best was brave, headstrong Saint Peter, so weak at first, so firm and faithful at last. And next he loved the kind Saint John with his great loving heart and gentle kindly ways. These two dream friends were far more real to him than any of the gay companions among whom he lived, and it is little wonder that the boy prince with such friends kept himself pure and unspotted from the world and earned the title of "Confessor."

The only thing outside his dream life in which Prince Edward delighted was in the chase. After long hours spent in church he would gallop off for days into the forest, hunting and hawking, no longer a dreamy youth with downcast eyes, but a keen alert sportsman whose eyes shone with daring and excitement.

It was while hunting one day that his horse stumbled on the edge of a dangerous cliff, and, with a swift appeal to his unseen friend, the Prince called upon Saint Peter to save him.

"Saint Peter," he cried, "save me, and I vow that I will make a pilgrimage to thy shrine in Rome to mark my gratitude."

The stumbling horse recovered its foothold and Edward rode safely home. Going straight to church, he knelt there giving thanks for his safety, and while he was still on his knees there came a messenger from England bidding him return and rule over the people as their rightful King.

This good fortune made him more anxious than ever to keep the vow he had made that day. The saint had been his friend and helper in the time of exile, and now, when fortune smiled upon him, he longed to show his gratitude the more.

But Edward had soon to learn that a king belongs to his people and not to himself.

As soon as it was known that the new king desired to make a pilgrimage to Rome, the people were dismayed and horrified.

"We cannot allow it," they cried. "A king can only leave his kingdom with the consent of the Commons, and that consent we will not give."

The wise councillors and advisers also shook their heads.

"The risks are too great," they said. "There are perils by road and sea, by mountain pass and river, dangers from robbers and armed foes. Who would venture among those Romans who are such villains, caring only for the red gold and the white silver?"

So it was that the King was sorely troubled that day as he sat and thought of all these things. He had sent messengers to Rome to beg that he might be pardoned for breaking his vow, and now he was awaiting their return, wondering what answer the Pope would send.

SAINT EDWARD THE CONFESSOR

Ere long the answer came, and the Pope's message cheered Edward's heart. Instead of making a pilgrimage to Rome to do honour to Saint Peter, the King was to show his gratitude by building or restoring some monastery belonging to Saint Peter, which should be for ever after under the special protection of the Kings of England.

It was a happy way out of the difficulty, and the King began at once to consider where the abbey should be built. He was deep in thought one day, sitting with his head resting on his hand, his dreamy eyes already seeing visions of a wonderful minster pointing its spires heavenward, when a servant entered and told him that a holy man, a hermit, begged to be allowed speech with the King.

"Bring him hither at once," said Edward; "it is not fit that a holy man should be kept waiting."

It was very trying to be interrupted when his whole heart was filled with thoughts of the great plan, but he put them aside and turned to give a kindly greeting to the old man, who had perhaps come to ask a boon of his King. He little guessed that this very interruption was to bring him the help which he sought.

Very slowly and with trembling steps the old hermit came into the royal presence. King's palaces were strange abodes to one who lived in the caves and rocks of the earth. The green boughs of the trees were the only canopy which the old man knew; the daisied grass was his carpet, and for companions he had the squirrels and the birds, with whom he shared his meal of fruit and roots. But God had sent His servant with a message and he was here to deliver it to the King. The strange city, the bewildering noise, and the wonderful palace were things which had nought to do with him. His one desire was to tell his tale. The King listened with earnest attention, for the message was a strange one.

"Three nights ago," said the hermit, "as I knelt at prayer, behold there appeared to me in a vision an old man, bright and beautiful like to a clerk, whom I knew to be Saint Peter. He bade me tell thee that thou wouldst even now be released from thy vow, and commanded instead to build an abbey. The place where thou shouldst build the abbey, said he, should be on the Isle of Thorns, two leagues from the city. There a little chapel of Saint Peter already stands, and there the great abbey shall be built, which shall be indeed the Gate of Heaven and the Ladder of Prayer. As soon as the vision was ended I wrote all the words down upon this parchment, sealed it with wax, and now have brought it to your Majesty."

So the spot was chosen on which the fair abbey should be built, and King Edward gave his whole heart and attention to the great work.

The little Isle of Thorns of which the hermit spoke had taken its name from the wild forest and thickets with which it was overgrown. It was also called the "Terrible Place" in the days when it was the refuge for the wild animals which came down from the hills around. In those days it was said that a heathen temple had been built on the island, and that later, in the time of King Sebert, it had been turned into a Christian chapel and dedicated to Saint Peter.

Now there was a curious old legend about the dedication of that little chapel in the midst of the wild thicket of thorns, and perhaps it helped the dreamy King to decide to build his abbey there.

The legend tells that in the days of King Sebert, when the monastery was finished, it was arranged that on a certain day Mellitus, the first Bishop of London, should consecrate the chapel. It so happened that, the night before the consecration, a fisherman named Edric was casting his nets into the Thames from the Isle of Thorns when, on the opposite shore, he saw an old man, who hailed him and asked that he might be rowed across to the little island. The old man was dressed in a curious foreign robe and seemed to be a stranger, but he had a beautiful kindly face, and Edric willingly did his bidding. Across the dark stream they rowed, and when the old man landed on the island, Edric stood watching to see where he would go.

The stranger walked straight to the chapel door, and as he entered, lo! the whole chapel was flooded with a blaze of light, so that it stood out fair and shining without darkness or shadow. Then a host of angels, swinging their golden censers, began to descend from above and to ascend, linking earth with heaven, and the sweet blue breath of the incense trailed in thin clouds around the brightness of the heavenly torches. Slowly and solemnly the service of consecration was performed, while the awe-struck fisherman, forgetting his nets and his fishing, gazed in wonder at the heavenly vision.

Presently the lights faded, the angels vanished, and the little chapel was left in darkness once more. Then the old man came out of the chapel and greeted the wondering fisherman.

"How many fish hast thou taken?" asked the stranger.

Edric stammered out that he had caught no fish, and the old man smiled kindly upon him, seeing his confusion.

"To-morrow thou shalt tell the Bishop Mellitus all thou hast seen," he said. "I am Peter, Keeper of the Keys of Heaven, and I have consecrated my own church of Saint Peter, Westminster. For thyself, go on with thy fishing, and thou shalt catch a plentiful supply. This I promise thee on two conditions. First, that thou shalt no more fish on Sundays; and secondly, that thou shalt pay a tithe of the salmon to the abbey of Westminster."

Early next day came the Bishop Mellitus to consecrate the chapel, as he had arranged, and the first to meet him was the fisherman Edric, who stood waiting there with a salmon in his hand. He told his tale, and presented his salmon from Saint Peter, and then showed the Bishop where the holy water had been sprinkled, and all the signs of the heavenly consecration.

The Bishop bowed his head in reverence as he listened, and prepared to return home.

"My services are not needed," he said: "the chapel hath indeed been consecrated in a better and more saintly fashion than a hundred such as I could have consecrated it."

In the days of King Edward the Isle of Thorns was no longer the Terrible Place, for the forest had been cleared and Saint Peter's chapel stood in the midst of flowery meadows; but still the fishermen cast their nets in the river and caught many a silver salmon, and once a year Saint Peter's fish was carried to the monastery in payment of the tithe which Edric had promised.

There were two other legends told of the little chapel which seem to have made King Edward love the place with a special love.

One story tells how a poor cripple Irishman named Michael sat one day by the side of the path which led to the chapel, watching for the King to pass. The kindly King at once noticed the lame man, and stopped to talk to him. Michael with piteous earnestness told his tale, and begged for help. There seemed no cure for his lameness, although he had made six pilgrimages to Rome, but at last Saint Peter had promised that he would be cured if only the King would carry him up to the chapel upon his own royal shoulders.

The courtiers mocked, and turned their backs on the ragged beggar, but King Edward, with kind compassionate words, bent down and lifted the cripple, and carried him up to the chapel, where he laid him before the altar. Immediately strength returned to the poor crippled limbs: the man stood upright, then knelt and thanked God and his King, and blessed the little chapel of Saint Peter.

The other legend tells of a wonderful vision sent to bless the eyes of the Confessor in the same chapel, as he knelt before the altar. Perhaps it was because his heart was pure and innocent and his faith so strong that his earthly eyes were opened to see the Christ-Child Himself standing there "pure and bright like a spirit," while a glory shone around.

It was small wonder, then, that the King was glad to choose this spot on which to build a great abbey to the glory of God and Saint Peter. The work was begun at once, and the King came to live in the palace of Westminster that he might be near at hand and watch the building. A tenth part of all the wealth of the kingdom was spent upon the abbey, and it took fifteen years to build; but the King grudged neither time nor money in carrying out this, his heart's desire. Indeed the King had but little idea of the value of money, and was sometimes rather a trial to his steward Hugolin, who had charge of the chest where the royal gold was kept. Sometimes Hugolin lost all patience with his royal master, and shook his head over his dreamy ways.

Why, there had been one day when Edward had actually encouraged a thief to steal his gold! The money-chest had been left open in the King's room, and a scullion from the kitchen had come creeping in thinking the King was asleep. Edward had watched the thief help himself three times to the gold, and then had warned him to make haste and get away before Hugolin should return.

"He will not leave you even a halfpenny," cried the King, "so be quick."

The words only added to the scullion's terror, as he gazed upon the white-haired King who was watching him so intently. He fled from the room, glad to take the King's advice and to escape before the steward's return.

"Your Majesty has allowed yourself to be robbed," said Hugolin reproachfully, when he saw the empty chest and heard the King's story.

"The thief hath more need of it than we," said his master; "enough treasure hath King Edward."

The King's treasure was indeed spent lavishly upon the building of the great abbey, and soon it began to rise from its foundations like a flower, growing in beauty and stateliness year by year, while the dreamy King watched over it, and added every beauty that his fancy could devise. Rough grey stone was cut and sculptured into exquisite shapes and designs; the daylight, as it streamed through the rich stained glass of the windows, was turned as if by magic into shafts of purest colour—purple, crimson, and blue. Fair as a dream the abbey stood finished at last, built by a dweller in dreamland, but solid and firm as a rock upon its foundations, and as firmly to be fixed in the hearts of the English people, while they ever weave around it their dreams of all that is great and good—the honour and glory of England.

The King's life was drawing to a close just as the great abbey was completed, and Edward knew that this was so. All his life he had relied greatly on warnings and visions, and now strange tales were told of how the end had been foretold.

It was said that as the King was on his way to the dedication of a chapel to Saint John, he was met by a beggar who asked alms of him.

"I pray thee help me, for the love of Saint John," cried the beggar.

Now the King could not refuse such a request, for he loved Saint John greatly. But he had no money with him and Hugolin was not at hand, so he drew off from his finger a large ring, royal and beautiful, and gave it with a kindly smile to the poor beggar.

Not very long afterwards, the legend tells us, two English pilgrims far away in Syria lost their way, and wandered about in darkness and amidst great dangers, not knowing which road led to safety. They were almost in despair, when suddenly a light shone across their path, and in the light they saw an old man with bowed white head and a face of wonderful beauty.

"Whence do ye come?" asked the old man, "and what is the name of your country and your King?"

SAINT EDWARD THE CONFESSOR

"We are pilgrims from England," replied the wanderers, "and our King is the saintly Edward, whom men call the Confessor."

Then the old man smiled joyously, and led them on their way until they came to an inn.

"Know ye who I am?" he asked. "I am Saint John, the friend of Edward your King. This ring which he gave for love of me, ye shall bear back to him, and tell him that in six months we shall meet together in Paradise."

So the pilgrims took the ring and carried it safely over land and sea until they reached the King's palace, when they gave it back into the royal hand and delivered the message from Saint John.

It was midwinter when the abbey was ready for consecration. The river ran dark and silent as on that long-ago night when the fisherman rowed Saint Peter across to the little chapel and the angels came to sing the service. Now all that earthly hands could do was done, and the greatest in the land were gathered there to be present at the consecration of Saint Peter's abbey. Only the King was absent. He who had dreamed the fair dream and wrought it out in solid stone and fairest ornament, was lying sick unto death while the seal was set upon his work.

For a few days he lingered on, and then from the land of dreams he passed to the great Reality, and the old chronicles add the comforting words: "Saint Peter, his friend, opened the gate of Paradise, and Saint John, his own dear one, led him before the Divine Majesty."

They laid the King to rest in the centre of his beautiful abbey, and, ever since, our land has held no greater honour for her heroes than to let them sleep by the resting-place of the saintly King.

All honour to those who, through the might of sword or pen, by courage or learning, have won a place within Saint Peter's abbey of Westminster! But for the simple of the earth it is good to remember, that he who was first laid there won his place not by great deeds of courage or gifts of wondrous learning, but by the simple faith that was in him, the kindly thought for those who were poor and needed his help, the loving-kindness which even a child may win, though he miss a hero's grave in the King's abbey.

SAINT COLUMBA

THE Princess Eithne lay asleep, dreaming of summer days and happy hours spent in flowery meadows. Outside the stormy wintry winds swept the snow-drifts high among the mountain passes, and the howls of hungry wolves mingled with the shriek of the wind. It was cold and bleak at the castle of Gartan among the wild hills of Donegal when winter held sway, and then the Princess would watch the swirling snowflakes and the grey mists that wrapped the hills in solemn majesty. But in the springtime it was a different world, and Eithne could see from her window the length and height of the valley, and count the little mountain lakes that shone like diamonds in their emerald setting, and she thought it was the fairest spot in all the world.

There were so many beautiful things in the life of the Princess, so much to make her happy with the Prince her husband, that there seemed scarcely room for more joy; and yet, as she lay dreaming, she knew that the greatest happiness of all was yet to come.

It seemed to her that, as she dreamed of those flowery meadows, an angel stood beside her and placed in her hands a wonderful robe, more beautiful than anything she had ever seen. It was sewn all over with dainty flowers—the mountain flowers that are fairer and finer than any others because they grow closer to heaven. It was as if a rainbow had fallen into a shower of flowers upon this wondrous mantle and set it thick with buds and blossoms, crimson, white, and blue.

For a space the angel waited while the Princess held the robe and gazed upon its beauty, then very gently it was taken from her and Eithne found her hands were empty.

"Why dost thou take away my beautiful robe so soon?" asked the Princess, stretching out her hands towards the angel and weeping bitterly.

"It is too dearly prized for thee to keep it," was the answer. And as Eithne looked with longing eyes, she saw the angel spread out the robe, and its beautiful folds floated further and further until it covered all that land.

Then in her ears there sounded the comforting voice of the angel bidding her grieve no more, but prepare to receive the little son whom God was sending to her. And Eithne knew that the vision of the robe was sent as a lesson to teach her that her son would belong not only to her but to the world, where God had need of him.

Soon after this the little Prince was born, and, as his mother held him in her arms, her heart was filled with the same great joy as when she had clasped the angel's robe. More than fifty years had passed since the good Saint Patrick had brought

Christ's light to Ireland, and now most of the people there were Christians. The father and mother of the little Prince took early care that the baby should be baptized, and in the little chapel of the clan O'Donnel they gave him two names—Crimthann, which means a wolf, and Colum, which means a dove.

Perhaps it was the chief, his father, thinking of his wild brave ancestors living free among those mountains, who gave his little son the name of the wolf, and surely it was the mother, thinking of the angel vision, who wished him to be called by the gentler name.

There was no doubt from the first which name suited the child the best. Strong and fearless, and showing in a hundred ways that he came of a kingly race, there was nothing of the wild wolf nature about Columba. It was always Colum, the dove, that gladdened his mother's heart. Like a flower turning to the light, his heart seemed always to turn naturally to all that was beautiful and pure and good. He was eager to learn, and loved to listen to the stories of those soldiers of Christ who fought against the Evil One, and brought light and peace into the wild dark places of the earth. When he grew up, he too would become one of those soldiers, and meanwhile there was nothing he loved so much as to steal away into the little chapel to join in the service of the Master he meant to serve some day.

The people wondered as they watched the boy leave his games and turn with a happy eager face towards the church whenever the bell called the monks to prayer.

"He should be called Columkill, Colum of the Church," they said: and so it was that the old name of "the dove of the Church" was first given to Columba.

At the monastery school the boy was quick to learn, and the monks told one another that he had the gift of genius. But the master, Saint Finnian, wondered even more at the goodness than the cleverness of his pupil. Watching him one day, he was heard to say that he saw an angel walking by the side of Columba, guiding and guarding him as he went. And, indeed, the boy's face had ever the look of one who walked close to his guardian angel.

So Columba grew to be a man, and learned all the wisdom of the great monasteries, and then, strong and purposeful, he began his work for God, going throughout the land teaching, and founding monasteries and building churches.

But although he worked well and with all his heart, still his great desire had always been to carry God's message of peace and goodwill to the heathen lands outside Ireland, and many a time did he gaze across the sea to the faint blue line of distant hills, thinking of those poor souls in Scotland who knew nothing of God's love and mercy.

Still the years went by, and there always seemed more than enough work for him to do in his own land until, when he was more than forty years

SAINT COLUMBA

old, something happened which changed his life, and sent him forth to begin the new great work.

Now you must know that Columba loved books and delighted in making copies of them, for in those days all books were written by hand. He was very skilful in this work of copying. He laid the colours on most carefully for the capital letters, and made the printing black and firm and even. Nothing gave him more pleasure than to have a new book to copy, and he was greatly pleased when one day he heard that his old master Saint Finnian had a wonderful copy of the gospels, and might allow him to see it.

"My father," he said to the old abbot, "I would that I might see the fair copy of the gospels of which I have heard so much. Men say there is no other copy like it in Ireland."

"Ay, my son," answered the abbot proudly, "it is, as thou sayest, a very fair copy. But thou hast a careful hand and knowest the value of such a book, so I will trust the treasure to thee for a space."

Overjoyed at the permission, Columba carried the book carefully home, and the more he looked at it, the more he longed to have one like it. At last he began secretly and swiftly to make a copy, and not until it was done did he return the precious book to Saint Finnian.

Before long, however, the matter came to the ears of the abbot, and he was very angry. He demanded at once that the copy should be given up, and bade Columba deliver it immediately.

"The copy is mine," said Columba calmly, "but if thou thinkest it is thine, we will let the King decide."

So the matter was taken to the King of Meath, and he decided that Columba must give up the book.

"It is written in the ancient law of our land," said the King, "that to every cow belongs its calf, therefore it must be that to every book belongs its copy."

There was a great outcry against this decision, and the clansmen of Columba went out to do battle with the men of Meath, and by the time Columba's anger had cooled, many thousand men had been killed.

Bitterly repentant, Columba went to the old priest Molaise, and asked him what he should do to show his sorrow. Then Molaise bade him leave the land he so dearly loved, cross the sea to Scotland, and win for God from among the heathen as many souls as those whom his hasty quarrel had brought to death.

The long waves of the Atlantic rolled in and broke upon the beach, grey and cold in the light of early morning, when twelve sorrowful-looking men pushed off their frail boats from the Irish shore, and set sail for distant Scotland.

The boats were light, made only of wickerwork with skins stretched tightly over, and they rose gaily on the long waves which came sweeping in as if eager to overwhelm them. But there were heavy hearts in those light boats, and the men looked back with sad eyes at the dear green home they were leaving, seeing it but dimly through a mist of tears. They loved their home, but they loved their master Columba better, and so they were setting sail with him for the land of exile.

Through storm and tempest the frail boats held their way, and the hearts, if sad, were brave and hopeful too, for their faith was strong in God and in their leader.

The first landing-place was on the island of Colonsay, and there the little company waited on the shore while Columba climbed the hill, that he might view the land and see if it was a fit place to make their home.

With long strides he climbed up over rocks and heather until at last he reached the top, and then he stood quite still and looked around him. Yes, the island was just the kind of resting-place he was seeking, since he must no longer live in his own dear land. Lifting up his eyes then, he gazed longingly across the blue sea in the direction of home, and his heart leaped when he saw in the distance the faint blue hills of Erin. Then he sighed, and went slowly back to his waiting companions.

"We must push on," he said. "If we stay here our hearts will be filled with a sore home-longing whenever we gaze across the sea. We must go further, where we cannot see the hills of home."

So the boats were pushed off once more, and the men rowed on until they reached the little island of Hy or Iona. Not the faintest trace of the blue Irish hills could be seen from here, so it was decided that this was to be the place where they would make their new home.

The warm May sunshine was flooding the island as the boats were pulled high on the shore. Sunbeams sparkled on the deep blue waves, and the shining sand of the little bay was dazzling in its whiteness. The sea-birds, disturbed in their loneliness, swooped and screamed over the heads of the new-comers, but there was nobody else to dispute their possession.

Very soon the building of the new home was begun. Columba, tall and strong, with clever hands and clever brain, planned and worked himself, and directed the others. One by one the huts were finished and the little chapel built, and then the monastery was complete. The King of that part of the country, knowing Columba, gave him the island for his own, and so there was no fear that the monks would be disturbed. There were other sounds now besides the screaming of sea-birds to be heard on Iona. There was the chapel bell calling the brothers to prayer; there was the music of the morning and evening hymns, and the cheerful busy sounds of daily work.

Then when all was set in order—fields prepared for harvest, cows brought over to give milk, and everything arranged for the daily life—Columba set out to begin the great work he had planned.

Far in the north lived the pagan King Brude, in a country where no Christian foot had ever trod. He was a strong and powerful King, and he sat in his grey northern castle fearing no man, for there was no army strong enough to march against him, and no one dared to withstand his power.

Who then were these strangers who came so boldly up to the gates and demanded an entrance? They were not soldiers, for they carried no weapons; they wore only robes of coarse homespun, and their shaven heads were uncovered. Yet they bore themselves with a fearless air, and their leader spoke in a voice that seemed accustomed to command. Like a trumpet-call the words rang out, "Open the gates in the name of Christ."

"The gates shall not be opened," swore the King. "These men are workers of magic and of evil. Keep the gates barred."

Then the leader, who was Columba, lifted his head still higher, and those who saw him wondered at the look that shone on his face, while the brothers, seeing that look, were cheered and encouraged as if they too could see the angel who stood near and guided him.

There was a breathless silence as the people waited to see what the strange man would do next, and they saw him slowly lift his hand on high and make the sign of the cross. At that sign, as if opened by unseen hands, the gates swung back, the guards fled to right and left, and the way was clear for Columba to enter. Not as an enemy or the worker of evil magic, as the King had feared, did the great man come, but rather as a dove bearing the olive-branch of God's peace.

And as the gates of iron had opened to God's servant, so the gates of the King's heart were unlocked as he listened to the words of Columba's message. The victory which no earthly force and weapons could win, was won by God's unarmed messenger alone. The King and many of his people were baptized, and the banner of Christ floated over the heathen citadel.

But although the King had become a Christian, there were still many people who hated Columba and his religion. The Druids, priests of the heathen religion, were very angry, and tried in every way to harm this man who had brought a new religion into their country. They could not bear to see the people listening to his teaching, and when it was time for evensong and the brethren were singing their evening hymn of praise, these Druids strove to drown the sound by making hideous noises and raising a terrible din. Little did they know the strength of that voice against which they were striving. Loud and clear rose the hymn of Columba, swelling into a great burst of praise which throbbed through the air and could be heard a mile away. Each word sounded distinctly, and it drowned the evil sounds of those pagan priests, and rose up to heaven as clear and pure as the song of a lark.

Wherever Columba preached and taught he also built a little church, and left behind some of the brethren to go on with the work of spreading God's light. So through all the land there was a chain of churches and the light grew ever brighter and brighter.

But it was always to Iona that Columba returned, and which he made his home. There he worked and prayed and gathered fresh strength to fight the good fight. There in his cell he made fair copies of the books he loved, and was ready to help any one who came to him for advice and counsel. He was so kindly and patient, this great saint, that he never lost his temper, even when the visitors came and interrupted his work with unnecessary questions, and in their eagerness to embrace him knocked over his ink-horn and spilt his ink.

There was much work to be done by the brothers of the monastery besides their life of prayer and praise. There was the corn to be sown, the harvest to be reaped, cows to be tended, and there was also a seal farm to be cared for on one of the islands close by, where young seals were reared.

"Cross now to the island of Mull," said Columba one day, "and on the open ground near the sea search for the thief Ere, who secretly came last night from the island of Colonsay. During the day he is trying to hide himself among the sandhills under his boat covered with hay, in order that he may cross over to the little island where our young seals are reared, and there, filling his boat with those he has cruelly slain, may return to his own dwelling."

THERE IN HIS CELL HE MADE FAIR COPIES
OF THE BOOKS HE LOVED

In great haste the brothers set out, and very angry they were when they found this Ere skulking beneath his boat, just as Columba had said. They dragged him to their master with no gentle hands, and waited grimly for him to receive the punishment he deserved.

But the kindly eyes of the abbot only looked sorrowfully at the thief.

"Why dost thou transgress the divine command so often and steal the things of others?" he asked, "Whenever thou art in want come to us, and thou shalt receive whatever needful things thou askest."

Then he ordered that he should be given food. The thief stood with downcast eyes, more truly punished than the brethren knew, and after that the young seals were left in peace.

Among the many travellers who came to Iona to see Columba and to be entertained at the monastery, there were sometimes kings and nobles of high degree, but their coming did not move the abbot as did the arrival of a single poor guest, for whom he would bid the brethren prepare a special welcome. In the midst of all his work he still had time to care for the weak and helpless of God's creatures. Calling one of the brothers to his cell, he gave him his directions.

"At the dawn of the third day from this," he said, "when sitting on the shore of the sea on the western side of the island, I would have thee keep careful watch. For a crane, a stranger from the northern part of Ireland, driven about by the winds through long flights, will come after the ninth hour of the day. It will be fatigued and very weary, and with its strength almost spent will light on the shore and lie down before thee. Treat it tenderly and carry it to a neighbouring house, and there, when it hath been kindly received, do thou house and feed it three days and three nights. Then when refreshed after the three days' rest, it is unwilling to tarry longer with us, it will return with renewed strength to the pleasant part of Ireland from which it came. I earnestly commend it to thee, because it cometh from our own native place."

The brother did as Columba bade him, and when the crane arrived, weary and spent, he carried it in his arms to a safe shelter and tended it until the third day, when it was once more strong and well. Then the happy bird prepared for its homeward flight, and rising ever higher and higher in the air, searched out its way and flew straight for home, strengthened and refreshed by its visit to the saint, just as many a human heart, fainting and sore, won healing from that same kindly heart.

As time went on, Columba returned once or twice to Ireland; but he never stayed there long, for his heart was in his work and the "Island Soldier" was ever in the forefront of the battle.

It was once, when he was visiting the monastery of Saint Ceran in Ireland, that a great crowd came out to meet him, and the monks were obliged to shelter him under a wooden frame to prevent the people from pressing too closely upon him. There were all kinds of people in the crowd, rich and poor alike, all eager to reach the saint and receive his blessing, and among them was a poor boy belonging to the monastery. Now this boy, living as he did amongst the good brothers, ought to have learnt to be clean and neat, obedient and diligent, but that was exactly what he was not. His face and hands were grimy and dirty; his clothes were torn and untidy; he scarcely ever did what he was told to do; and he never did any work that he could possibly help doing. You would not have thought that any good was hidden away under all that naughtiness, any more than you would think that a pearl could be hidden in an ugly oyster shell. But yet the pearl was there.

This boy, whose name was Ernene, pressed through the crowd that day with half-idle curiosity to see the saint, but when he caught a glimpse of that kind beautiful old face, a wild longing filled his heart. Beneath all his naughtiness there had always been a longing after good and beautiful things, and he had dreamed dreams of doing brave and noble deeds and following some great leader. Here then was the leader he had dreamed of, and the sight of his face woke up all the old desires after goodness and a noble life. But it was all so difficult. He was only a poor boy, with no strength to fight against the snares of the Wicked One, no hope of coming out victor in the fight. Surely though, if he could but get near enough to the saint to touch his robe, some of the wonderful strength the saint possessed might be given to him.

Slowly, then, he crept behind the moving figure, ever nearer and nearer, until at last one grimy little hand was stretched out, and caught for a moment the hem of Columba's robe. It was a swift movement, but the saint was quicker still, and with a sudden swing of his arm he turned and caught the boy by the back of his neck and swung him round in front.

There was an instant halt, and angry voices rose from those around. "Let him go, let him go," they cried. "Why touch that unhappy naughty lad?" But no one dared to thrust the child away while Columba's hand still held him close. "Suffer it, brethren," said Columba gently; "suffer it to be so now."

Then he looked down at the poor little quaking form, shaken with terror and confusion. "My son," he said suddenly, "open thy mouth and put out thy tongue."

The boy obeyed instantly. The saint might mean to punish him in some dreadful way, but he was ready to do whatever that voice commanded.

But Columba had seen the shining pearl lying deep down in that little black heart, and he knew of that longing to do noble deeds. Very kindly he smiled into the frightened eyes of the child, and raised his hand, not to strike but to bless. Then he turned to the monks who stood wondering round.

"Though this lad now appears to you vile and worthless," he said, "let no one on that account despise him; for from this hour he shall not only not displease you, but shall greatly delight you. From day to day he shall gradually advance in good conduct, and great shall be his progress in your company. Moreover, to his tongue shall be given of God sound and learned eloquence."

There was no more carelessness, no more disobedience, no more idleness for Ernene after this. Day by day, everything evil and ugly that hid the pearl of good desire was gradually cleared away, and the boy grew to be one of the best and greatest of those who served God in the monastery. There was many a fight before the Evil One was beaten, but the tongue blessed by Columba learned to speak only the words that were true and kindly and pure, and like the helm of a ship, although it was but a little thing, yet it held command over the whole body.

There is no room to tell of all the wonders and brave deeds and kindly acts of Saint Columba. It seemed as if there was nothing that he could not do, for he always believed that God would answer his prayers. When his servant Diomit was dying, Columba knelt by his bedside and prayed for his life, and the life was given back. When the brethren were out one day on a stormy sea in one of the frail hide-covered boats, it was again Columba's prayers that saved them. He had worked with all his might baling out the water, while the waves dashed over the side of the boat and threatened every moment to sink it.

"Pray to God for us," cried the brethren. "That is our only hope."

Then Columba stood up, drenched and blinded by the spray, and he stretched his hands out to heaven and prayed to the Master who once, in a little fishing-boat with His disciples, had met just such a storm as this. And as he prayed, in an instant the answer came. Winds and waves, as of old, knew when to obey the voice of command, and "there was a great calm."

Like his Master, too, Columba loved to seek some lonely quiet place where he could spend the time in prayer, and the place he loved best was the little hill behind the convent. The brothers sometimes wondered why he stayed there so long, and once it happened that one of them, filled with curiosity, climbed up secretly to see what their abbot was doing. But the sight that he saw there put his prying eyes to shame, for it was a vision of angels that met his gaze. There, around the praying form of Columba, God's white-robed messengers hovered, waiting to carry his prayers up to the throne of God. So it is that the place is called the "Angels' Hill" to this day.

The years passed by and Columba, growing old and frail, knew that his work was nearly done and the end drawing nigh. He had half hoped that at Eastertide God would call him home, but knowing that the Easter joy of the others would then be turned into sadness, he waited patiently for God's good time.

The month of June had come. The island looked its fairest, decked in tender greens and embroidered with late spring flowers. The sea was at its bluest under the cloudless sky, and everything spoke of life and joy. But the hearts of the brethren in the monastery were heavy and sad. Each day they saw their beloved abbot growing more and more feeble, and they too knew the end was near. His steps now were slow and painful, and it was with difficulty that he made his way to the granary to bless the corn, as was his wont. As he went he leaned upon the shoulder of his faithful servant Diomit, but even then he could go but slowly; and coming back he sat down to rest at the wayside, for he was very weary. The white horse belonging to the monastery came by as he sat there, and seeing its master, stopped and looked with wise, sorrowful eyes at the tired figure resting by the roadside. All animals loved Columba, and many a kind word and handful of corn had this horse received from the master's hand as it daily carried the milk pails to the monastery.

But to-day, in some curious way, the white horse saw the shadow of death which was already beginning to steal up over the waning life of the saint, and it came nearer and nearer until it nuzzled its head in Columba's bosom, giving little whinnying cries of distress while the tears filled its eyes. Diomit would have driven the creature off, but Columba would not allow that.

"Suffer him, since he loves me," he said, "to pour out his grief into my bosom. Thou, though thou art a man, could in no way have known of my departure if I had not told thee, but to this animal the Creator in His own way has revealed that his master is about to leave him."

Then, slowly rising, Columba lifted his hand and blessed the horse as it stood there with sorrowful hanging head.

Before returning home, the saint, weary as he was, climbed once more the little hill he loved, and there, looking down upon the monastery, he blessed it in words that have been carried down through all the years.

"To this place," he said, "small and mean though it be, not only the Kings of the Scots with their peoples, but also rulers of strange and foreign nations and their subjects, shall bring great honour in no common measure, and by the saints of other churches shall no slight reverence be shown."

So the last blessing was given, and the work almost finished. Only a few verses of the Psalms remained to be copied, and these Columba sat writing when he returned to his hut.

"They that seek the Lord shall want no manner of thing that is good."

Slowly and carefully the words were written, and the work was finished.

"Here I shall stop," he said, and the pen was laid aside for ever.

The summer twilight lingered on long after the crimson banners of the sinking sun had faded into grey. Then one by one the stars came out, and a deep silence brooded over the monastery. Suddenly, as midnight struck, the chapel bell rang out clear and sharp, and in an instant there was a stir among the little huts as the brothers prepared to answer the call to prayer. Swiftly then a tall grey figure came running towards the chapel and entered the door. Diomit, hurrying after, paused and looked up at the windows in amazement. The whole chapel was filled with a blaze of light, and the glory was reflected in every window. What could it mean?

Hastening on he reached the door, but when he entered the light had faded and all within was thick darkness.

"My father, my father, where art thou?" cried Diomit, as he groped his way in with trembling outstretched hands. Then, as his eyes grew more accustomed to the darkness, he dimly saw a figure lying silent and still before the altar. In a moment he was kneeling by Columba's side and raising him in his arms, while the rest of the brothers, bearing lights, came hurrying in.

There was a wild outburst of sobs and cries of grief as the brethren gathered round, but all sounds were hushed when they looked at the face of their dying master. It was no earthly joy that shone there, but a glory of shining happiness reflected from the angel faces which only his eyes could see. Diomit, praying for a last blessing, raised the master's hand, and as the sign was given, Columba's soul went home to God.

Kneeling round, the brothers sang the usual midnight service, their voices choked with sobs; and in their midst lay the quiet figure, the vision of angels still reflected upon the calm happy face.

SAINT MARGARET OF SCOTLAND

A GRAY sky overhead; a cold bitter wind sweeping the spray from off the crests of the great grey waves; a grey inhospitable-looking land stretching north and south. This was what the dim morning light showed to the eyes of the anxious watchers in the little boat which was battling its way along the shores of the Firth of Forth. Truly it was but a dark outlook, and the hearts of the little company on board were as heavily overshadowed by the clouds of misfortune, doubt, and foreboding, as the gloomy shores were wrapped in their folds of rolling mist.

It was a royal burden that the little boat bore up the waters of the Firth that wintry day of wind and mist. Edgar the Etheling, grandson of Edmond Ironside, driven from his kingdom by the all-conquering William, had fled northwards with his mother and two sisters, Margaret and Christina. Some faithful followers had thrown in their lot with the royal fugitives, but it was but a small company all told. No wonder that their hearts were heavy that wintry morning. Obliged to flee from their own country, driven out of their course by the raging tempest, what welcome awaited them in this bleak land, of which they had heard many a savage tale? Would they be treated as friends or looked upon as enemies? The royal family had meant to return to Hungary, where Edgar and his sisters had spent the days of their happy childhood, but the winds and waves had proved as furious and unkind as those subjects from whom they had fled, and there seemed nothing to do now but to seek some landing-place along the rocky shore, some shelter from the pitiless storm.

Among the weary, spent travellers there was one who was calm and untroubled, whose face reflected none of the gloom of the skies overhead, on whom the dreary foreboding of the future cast no shadow. Fair and stately as a lily the Princess Margaret stood gazing across the angry waters, marking the desolate rocky shores, watching the white sea-birds as they swooped and rose again, as confident and unruffled as one of those white birds herself. For Margaret knew that a greater than an earthly king was with her, and that He, her Lord and Master, held the grey waters and their uncertain fortunes in the hollow of His hand, able as ever to calm the winds and waves of this troublesome world with that comforting command, "Peace, be still."

"To the right, to the right," shouted a sailor on the look-out; "yonder is a little bay where methinks we should find shelter and means to land."

"Ay, if there be no rocks to guard the way," said the captain cautiously. But nevertheless he turned the boat landwards, and eager eyes scanned the shore as they approached. It seemed indeed a haven of refuge, a peaceful little bay, gathered in from the angry waters by a little wooded arm of land that guarded it so securely that the rough breakers went sweeping past, and the sandy beach sloped gently down to meet the little dancing waves, while the wet sand reflected the swooping white wings of the sea-birds that hovered about the shore.

The little company were thankful indeed to land at last, and to feel the firm earth under their feet once more. The mist too had begun to roll away, and a gleam of sunshine touched into warmer colour the bare hills around. Surely this was a good omen, and they might hope that the clouds of their evil fortune were also about to break. It is more than eight hundred years since that little company landed at the sheltered cove, and it might seem as if their very names were long since forgotten, but a faint memory of far-off romance is still linked to the place by the name it bears, Saint Margaret's Hope.

With weary steps the travellers began to journey inland, where they hoped to find some town or village close by. The few country people they met stared at them with round eyes of wonder. Who could these people be? They were without doubt of high rank. Even the King did not wear such fine garments. The beautiful ladies did not look fit to walk such rough roads. They must have landed from yon boat which lay in the cove beneath. The one thing to be done was certainly to hasten to the court and tell of the arrival of the strangers.

Up hill and down dale the little company journeyed on, until at last even Margaret's brave spirit grew weary, and she begged them to rest awhile in one of the green fields, where there was a great stone that would make a comfortable seat for the tired ladies. "Saint Margaret's Stone" the people call it still, and many a poor wayfarer, tired out with the tramp along dusty roads, sits and rests there now, as did the Princess Margaret long ago.

Perhaps in happier days afterwards, Margaret, looking back, may have often thought of that stone when she read the old story of Jacob and his stony pillow. Had not she, like him a weary fugitive driven from home, chosen a stone to rest upon? Had not a golden link with heaven been formed there too, and had not God's kind angels spread around her their tender care, leading her into the peaceful paths of light and happiness?

It was as they sat resting there that they were startled by the sound of many feet approaching, and a company of horsemen were seen coming towards them. Did they come as friends or enemies, was the swift thought that passed through each anxious mind. But fears were soon dispelled by the words of welcome that greeted them, and the rough men behaved themselves most reverently and courteously. They were come in the name of their King, Malcolm of Scotland, to bid the travellers welcome, they said. The royal palace close by at Dunfermline was at their disposal. Their lord himself was far away in England fighting against the usurper, but he would ere long be back to give them his own royal welcome.

So with lightened hearts and less weary feet the travellers went on, and soon caught sight of the town, built like an eagle's nest upon the steep hillside.

Now the King, Malcolm Canmore or Great Head, had made up his mind to befriend the fugitive Prince, and to uphold his cause against the usurping Norman. He himself knew what it meant to be a homeless wanderer, for when but a boy, the treacherous Macbeth had seized his kingdom, and it was by the strength of his own right arm and dauntless courage that he had won back his crown. He had never forgotten the kindness he had received at the Saxon court at the hands of Edward the Confessor, and perhaps there too he had seen the boy Edgar and his beautiful sister Margaret. Margaret's beauty was not a thing to be lightly forgotten, and the Scottish King, with his lionlike head and lionlike nature, had a large heart which was very easily touched by beauty of any kind.

It was soon seen, after the King's return to his palace at Dunfermline, that he loved the gentle Margaret with all the devotion of his great heart. She seemed to him something so precious, so delicately fair, that he hardly dared dream of winning her. It was like roughly plucking a harebell which had bravely lifted its head among the stones on his mountain path, linked to earth only by that slender stem which one rough touch might break. But he did most truly love her, and as his Queen he would be able to shield and guard from any harm the flower of his heart.

Margaret, however, was sorely troubled. This was not the life she had planned. She had thought to leave behind her the cares and troubles of a court, and to find peace and quietness in a convent home, where she might serve God. Far away in Hungary, where she had spent her childhood, and in the peaceful old home in England, she had loved to listen to stories of the lives of the saints, and especially had she pondered over the life of Saint Margaret, and longed to follow in her namesake's steps.

But there are more ways than one of serving God, and Margaret dimly saw that perhaps the path beset with most difficulties might be the one that her Master would have chosen. It would be sweet to serve Him in the peaceful shelter of a convent cell, but faithful and brave soldiers do not seek the safest posts, where duties are easy and dangers few. They seek to endure hardness and not ease. To be a good Queen might be a higher and more difficult task than to be a devout nun.

So Margaret at last consented to be wed, and when the first primroses were beginning to star the woods, and spring hastened to breathe a softer welcome to the English bride, the royal marriage took place at Dunfermline in the happy Eastertide.

But although the King had now attained the wish of his heart, he did not yet fully understand how pure and precious a gift had been bestowed upon him. Not very long after his marriage with Margaret, evil tongues began to whisper secret tales to which the King should never have given heed. They told how the Queen, when he was absent, stole out from the palace to meet his enemies in a certain cave not very far off in the woods.

Angry and suspicious, the King determined to find out the truth of the story, and one day, pretending to go out to the hunt, he returned secretly to the palace. With a heavy heart he watched his fair Queen quietly slip through the postern gate, and make her way through the woods to the fatal cave. He followed her silently, and when she disappeared, crept close to the opening and listened. Yes, it was true! A great wave of fury surged up in his heart as he heard the voice he loved so well speaking to some one inside the cave. Too angry to stir for a moment, he stood there listening to the words she spoke; but as he listened a look of bewilderment flashed across his face, the red flush of anger faded, and he hung his head as if ashamed. For the voice he heard was indeed Margaret's, but it was to God she spoke. "King and Lord of all," she prayed, "teach my dear King to serve Thee truly, to love Thee perfectly, and to walk in Thy light."

There were no more suspicious thoughts, no more listening to evil gossip after this, but the heart of Malcolm was bound more closely by the golden thread of love to his dear Queen, and thus through her was linked to God.

The news of the King's marriage with the beautiful English Princess was carried far and near, and the people wondered greatly what manner of Queen she would make. They watched her narrowly, and at first were not quite sure if her manners and customs were to their liking. Was it pride that made this great lady dress herself in such fair robes—kirtles of rainbow hue that hung in graceful folds, mantles all broidered with gay devices in colours borrowed from the peacock's plumes? Yet as they looked at their own strong useful garments, grey and dun-coloured as the wintry skies, they allowed that perhaps a little cheerful touch of colour might not come amiss.

Margaret's speech too was soft and courteous, and they were fain to confess that her graciousness won their hearts, almost in spite of themselves. But they were suspicious at first of all the changes at the court. Why, even the King himself began to show more kingly manners and to live in greater state. The servants no longer did their work in a slovenly way; the common drinking-cups and platters were replaced by silver goblets and golden dishes. The palace was royally furnished; all was fitly set out and well ordered. And yet the people very clearly saw that it could not be pride that made the gentle Queen insist on all this state. They soon found that a self-denying pitiful heart dwelt under her magnificent robes, that she was ready to give even her own garments to clothe the poor, and if she fed off a golden platter, the food was as simple as that of the humblest of the land. But she was a Queen, and the simple rule of her life was that all things should be fitly ordered. Neither in this did she stop at her own palace gates. The whole kingdom soon felt the influence of the hand that could guide even the great-headed Malcolm.

Many abuses had crept into the ancient Church, and Margaret longed to set these right. It must have been a strange sight to see the Queen in her beautiful robes, seated in the midst of all the clever men when they were gathered together to talk the matter over. If she was in earnest, so were they. Many a frowning black look was cast at the maiden who dared single-handed to do battle for the right. But Margaret loved her Church, and like Sir Galahad "her strength was as the strength of ten, because her heart was pure," and in the end she triumphed. Little by little, too, she taught her people that Sunday was a holy day, a day of rest for man and beast—a lesson sorely needed then, and never since forgotten.

So it seemed as if the love of God which dwelt in Margaret's heart was already bringing light into the dark places, and making the crooked ways straight, and she rejoiced to find that she could serve Him in the world as well as in the cloister.

It soon became known that any one in want or in trouble would find a friend in the new Queen. Her pitiful heart was linked to a helpful hand, and no one was ever turned empty away. Many were the ransoms she paid for poor English prisoners carried off captive in the fierce raids of the Scots. Widows and orphans flocked to the court, sure that the Queen would always befriend them in their distress.

Sometimes the King would laugh, and say that none of his possessions were safe from those hands that were so ready to give. When her purse was empty, the Queen would take off one of her own garments to clothe some shivering beggar, and when money was needed she would dip her hands into the King's private store of gold, well knowing that he grudged her nothing.

"Aha! I have caught thee now," he cried one day as he found her hurrying from his treasure-chest with well-filled hands. "What and if I have thee arrested, tried, and found guilty of robbery?"

Margaret smiled as she looked up into those kind laughing eyes.

"I plead guilty at once," she said, holding out the gold.

"Nay, dear heart," said the King, closing her fingers over the golden pieces. "Thou canst not steal what is already thine own. All that I have, thou knowest, is thine."

How truly the great rough King loved this gentle maiden! Everything she touched, everything she loved, was sacred to him. Often he would lift the books she had been using, and although he could not read the words she loved, he would hold the volumes lovingly in his great strong hands, and, half ashamed, would bend to kiss the covers which her hands had touched. Nothing, he thought, was quite good enough for his Queen. He could not bear that even the bindings of her books should be only of rough leather, and when he found a cunning worker in metals, he would have the covers overlaid with gold and precious stones, and with many a round white pearl, fit emblem of his Margaret, the Pearl of Queens.

It was one of these precious books, a book of the gospels, which Margaret loved above all the rest. Not only was its jewelled cover a token of the King's love, but the precious words inside were fitly illuminated with golden letters, and there were pictures of the four Evangelists most fair to look upon.

Now it happened that one day when Margaret was journeying from Dunfermline, a careless servant, who carried the book, let it slip from its wrappings into the midst of a river which they were fording. The man did not perceive that the book was lost, and thought no more of it until called upon by the Queen to deliver his precious burden. Long and sorrowfully he sought for it, retracing carefully each step he had come until at last he reached the river. Then he grew hopeless indeed. If it should have fallen into the stream, it would mean the end of the Queen's precious book. Ah! it was too true; there, in a clear stretch of water, where the ripples scarcely stirred the surface, he saw the gleam of white parchment as the leaves were gently stirred to and fro by the moving water. He bent down and lifted it carefully, and holding it safe in his hands, he gazed with wonder at the open leaves. The little coverings of silk which protected the golden letters had been loosened and swept away, but upon the pages themselves there was not a stain or blur. Not a single letter was washed out; the fair illuminated pictures were as clear and unspoiled as ever; the gold shone undimmed upon the pure white parchment leaves; the water had not injured one of the precious words of the Queen's book.

It was not only with money, her own or the King's, that Margaret helped the poor. She served them with her own hands as well. Early each morning the Queen, in her dainty robes, as fair as the dew-washed flowers that were just lifting their faces to the morning sun, came forth from her room, where she too had been lifting her face to heaven. It was her way to begin her daily work by caring for the little children who had no one else to care for them. Nine baby orphans were gathered there, poor and destitute, and it always seemed to her as if her Master was so close that she could almost hear His voice as He bade her "Feed My lambs." How joyfully the babies stretched out their hands towards her, clutching at the bonny coloured robe she wore with their little eager hands. All children love fair colours, but it was not only the green embroidered kirtle, no, nor the steaming breakfast which she brought, that made them stretch out their arms to her. There was a kind mother smile in her eyes which drew them to her as if by magic, and as she gathered them by turns into her loving arms, they were perfectly happy. Then the bowl of soft warm food was placed at her side, and one by one she fed each little orphan baby with her own golden spoon.

SAINT MARGARET OF SCOTLAND

ONE BY ONE SHE FED EACH ORPHAN WITH HER OWN GOLDEN SPOON

Later on each day there were gathered three hundred poor hungry people in the royal hall, and there the King, as well as the Queen, fed them and waited on them, giving to each the help they needed. Margaret never wearied of her work, for in helping the poor was she not waiting upon her Master? And as she knelt to wash the feet of some poor beggar, was she not washing the dust-stained weary feet of Him who had said—"Inasmuch as ye have done it unto one of the least of these my brethren, ye have done it unto Me."

But there was other work besides caring for the poor that filled Margaret's days. As time went on, God sent her children of her own to care for— six brave strong boys and two fair little maidens. Very carefully and very strictly were the children trained. Just because they were princes and princesses, they needed even more than others to learn to be obedient, gentle, brave and true. No one knew better than Margaret the truth of the old motto— "noblesse oblige." There is no denying that the children were sometimes naughty, as all children will be; and then indeed there was no sparing the rod, for the governor of the nursery was charged that they should be well whipped when they needed it.

There was an old castle not far from the royal palace, called in those days the Castle of Gloom, which the royal children knew well. Its name was fitly chosen, for well might it have been the dwelling of Giant Despair. High hills frowned down upon it, almost shutting out the light of the sun. At the foot of the steep precipice on which it was built two raging streams, called Dolor and Gryff, roared their way along, and helped to make the place more gloomy. It was to this castle that the child who had behaved ill and needed punishment was sent, that in dismal solitude he might learn to be sorry for his naughty ways. Not only the boys, but the little maidens too, learnt their lesson at the Castle of Gloom. It seemed strange and perhaps unkind that their gentle mother should have them whipped and sent away to the dark castle of punishment, but as they grew older and wiser, the children found that, strange as it had seemed, it was her very kindness and love that had made her punish them. Just as the hand of the gardener, who loves his garden, pulls up and destroys all the weeds, and prunes away everything that hinders the growth of his flowers, so the wise Queen tended her children, her special flowers. Thus it was that as her boys grew tall and strong and handsome, and her two little maidens became fair graceful women, it was not only the outward appearance that made such a brave show. In the garden of their hearts there were no evil weeds of selfishness, self-will and pride, but only the flowers of generosity, pity, self-forgetfulness, and the sovereign herb of obedience.

The gracious influence of the Queen was felt outside her household too, and the people around the court began to try and introduce the Queen's ways into their homes, and even to clothe themselves in gayer colours than their dull grey homespuns.

They were a hardy warlike people, as strong and rugged as their own grim grey mountain rocks, as wild and fearless as the mountain streams that came dashing down through the moorland waste.

But there are times when the mountains are no longer grim and grey, but tender and soft, in the blue haze that shows each peak against a primrose sky; when the mountain torrents sink into merry murmuring burns dancing along between the banks of fern and heather; when the bare moorlands are a glory of purple and gold as the heather merges into the autumn-tinted bracken. So these rugged northern folk had also their softer side, and deep in their hearts they felt the charm of fair colours and all things gracious and beautiful.

The merchants that came from all lands, bringing their wares at the bidding of the Queen, found the people eager and willing to buy. Indeed, it is said by some that it was this love of colour, introduced by Margaret, which was the origin of the Scottish tartans.

"But why," asked the Queen, "should we buy foreign wares? Why not weave these softer fairer stuffs ourselves?"

"The people know not the art of weaving such stuffs," replied her courtiers.

"Then they shall learn," replied the Queen. "They have as good brains and as deft hands as any of these foreigners, why should they not weave as well as others? I will see that my people are taught the art."

The Queen was as good as her word, and sent abroad for workers to teach her people at Dunfermline how to weave the fair white linen, giving them thus an industry which has lasted to this day.

But into this peaceful life of tending the poor, watching over her children and her people, sewing her wondrous embroideries and founding many churches to the glory of God, there came many a dreary time of anxiety and distress. Malcolm the King loved his peaceful home, but his strong brave arm was often needed to defend his country and protect his people, and many an anxious hour did Margaret spend while he went forth to fight the enemy. Her two elder boys, Edward and Edgar, went with their father now, and that made the anxiety even harder to bear.

Then came a time when it was more difficult than ever for Margaret to be brave and fearless. She was weak and ill, and the fear of some calamity seemed to hang around her like a thick cloud. It was in the month of June, when tardy Spring was in no haste to make room for her sister Summer, that the Queen sat alone in the castle of Edinburgh praying for the safe return of her dear King and their two brave sons. But yesterday they had set out with blare of trumpets and roll of drums to punish the invader who had dared to seize their castle of Alnwick, but already it seemed as if she had waited and watched for months.

Margaret did not greatly love the rugged castle of Scotland's capital. It was but a gloomy place compared to the dear home at Dunfermline, but still she made it homelike too. Its old name, the Maydyn or Maiden Castle, with its legend of Sir Galahad, pleased the Queen's fancy even if the place was somewhat rough. Often, as she sat gazing from the rocky height over the mist-wrapped town to where the line of the Forth showed like a silver thread, and across to where the great lion of Arthur's Seat and the Crags stood guard on one side of the city, she pictured the coming of the perfect knight. She saw him ride up the steep hillside and enter the ruined chapel there. She watched him as he knelt beside the altar praying for guidance, and heard too the voice that bade him ride on until he came to a great castle where many gentle maidens were imprisoned.

"There too thou shalt find a company of wicked knights," continued the voice. "Them thou shalt slay, and set the Maydyn Castle free."

The Maydyn Castle was but a rough home for Queen Margaret, but even there there were marks of her gracious presence. A little stone chapel was built upon the rock, and amidst the clang of weapons and sounds of war, the peaceful prayers of the Queen rose like sweet incense to heaven.

It was with difficulty that the Queen had managed to walk with feeble steps to the little chapel that sad June day; and as she prayed for the safety of her dear ones, who had ridden forth to meet danger and death, something seemed to tell her that they would never return. She felt as if even now misfortune was descending like a thick cloud upon the smiling land.

Her friend and counsellor Turgot, who writes the story of his Queen, tells how, when she had left the chapel, she turned to him and said with sad conviction: "Perhaps on this very day such a heavy calamity may befall the realm of Scotland as has not been for ages past."

It was while she was speaking these very words of sad foreboding that at the castle of Alnwick the heavy calamity had indeed fallen.

The gallant Malcolm with his two sons riding at the head of his men had reached the castle and called upon the garrison to surrender. The Scottish army was encamped below the castle, waiting to make the attack should the garrison refuse to yield. While they waited, a single unarmed knight rode out from the castle gate, carrying only his long spear, on the point of which hung the heavy keys of the castle stronghold.

"I come to surrender," he cried as he reached the camp. "Let your King come forth to receive at our hands the keys of his fortress."

There was no thought of treachery, and Malcolm with his visor up came out to meet the knight. As the King advanced the knight rode forward, and with a sudden swift movement, lowered his spear and drove its point straight into the eye of the King, piercing to his brain and killing him on the spot.

Then all was uproar and confusion. The infuriated Scots charged upon the enemy. Edward, the eldest son, rushing forward to avenge his father's death, was also slain. Little wonder that the heart that loved them both so dearly should feel the stroke, although far away.

With their King killed and their leaders gone, the Scottish soldiers lost heart, and were at last beaten back and utterly routed. There was no one left even to seek for the King's body, and it was left to two poor peasants to find it, and to carry it away in a cart to Tynemouth.

Four days passed before the news slowly travelled to the Maydyn Castle at Edinburgh, and it was Edgar, the second son, who brought the tidings to his dying mother.

She was lying peaceful and untroubled now, clasping in her hand that wonderful "Black Cross" which she loved so dearly. It was the cross which she had brought with her from England when she came a poor fugitive. Made of pure gold and set with great diamonds, it held in its heart something more precious still—a tiny splinter of her Lord's true Cross. It was her dearest possession, the most precious heirloom which she left to her sons, the youngest of whom, when he became King, "built a magnificent church for it near the city, called Holy-Rood."

The poor boy Edgar was almost heart-broken as he stood by his mother's bed. His father and brother were slain, enemies were already gathering round the castle, and his beloved mother lay here, sick unto death. He dared not tell her the direful news, lest it should snap the silver cord of life which already was worn so frail.

But his mother's eyes sought his, and he bent down to catch her feeble words.

"Is it well with thy father? Is it well with thy brother?"

"It is well," replied the boy bravely.

"I know it, my boy," she whispered with a sigh, "I know it. By this holy cross, by the bond of our blood, I adjure thee to tell me the truth."

Then the boy knelt by her side and very gently and tenderly told her the sad tidings. He need not have feared that the news would greatly trouble her. The veil had grown so thin that she could almost see into the glory beyond, and she knew that whatever her Master did was "well." A little while, and with a smile of great peace she welcomed the coming of the messenger of death, and to those who stood by it seemed as if they could feel the presence of God's angels as they stooped to bear away the soul of His faithful servant.

They robed the dead queen in the fairest of her royal robes, and there, in the rugged castle hall, she lay in state. Close around the castle thronged the enemies of the dead King, and those who greedily sought to snatch the crown from the fatherless boy.

It was well known that it had been the Queen's wish that her body should be laid to rest in the church she had built at Dunfermline, but every gate, every door of the castle was guarded and watched by the enemy, and it seemed as if the Queen's desire must remain unfulfilled. But men's strength is as nought when matched against Heaven's will.

Slowly there rolled up from the valley a dense grey fog, so thick that it blotted out everything in its heavy folds. The guards redoubled their watch at the gates, but there was one small postern door which they knew not of; and shrouded in the kindly mist, a little procession stole secretly through it, bearing the body of the Queen. Through the very midst of the enemy's lines the company passed in silence, unmolested and unseen. Behind them as they passed the mist closed in, and ere long they reached the banks of the Forth, at the landing-place called after Margaret, the Queen's Ferry. Then the friendly mist, no longer needed, lifted and rolled away, and the little company was able to cross the ferry and land at the bay of Margaret's Hope, the same little haven which had sheltered her, a fair young maiden, who now was carried home a loved and honoured Queen.

As the procession moved in haste towards Dunfermline many a poor peasant stole out and stood bareheaded to see her pass, many a voice was lifted in sorrowful wail to think those gentle hands which had so often cared for them were still for ever.

At last Dunfermline was reached in safety, and there, in her own beloved church, they laid the saint to rest.

SAINT MARGARET OF SCOTLAND

Long years have passed since that sad June day when they brought Queen Margaret's body home, but in the old churchyard, in what was once the Lady's Chapel, her tomb may still be seen, open now to the winds of heaven.

It is said that for many years after they laid her there to rest, flashes of light were seen glancing round the sacred spot, and that a sweet perfume as of flowers hung around the place, while those who were ill or in trouble were healed and helped by touching any relic of Saint Margaret. Whether that is but a legend we cannot tell, but this we know, that down the ages the light of her example and holy life has shone clear and steadily on, that the sweet perfume of her gentle deeds still lingers in the grey northern land which she so nobly helped to brighten and to beautify.

SAINT HUGH OF LINCOLN

EVIL days had fallen upon the little grey island of the north. Those who were strong used their strength to hurt the weak. Little heed was paid to law and order, and King Stephen's hands were too weak and helpless to govern a land that needed a strong stern ruler. Men said in their hearts, "God has forsaken England," for it seemed indeed as if the Evil One alone held sway.

But through the darkness there were faint signs of the coming dawn, and God's army was silently gathering strength to fight His battles and unfurl His banner.

Far away in the sunny land of France a little child was growing up at that time, knowing nothing and caring not at all about the woes of the little grey island of the north. Yet He who trains His saints to fight His battles was training the child to fight in many a hard struggle upon the battle-ground of England.

Little Hugh was born at the castle of Avalon near Grenoble, and was the son of a great noble to whom all Avalon belonged. Softly he was cradled and waited upon: the world was a place of sunshine and happiness to the son of the seigneur, and he had all that a child's heart could desire. But very soon a change came over his pleasant world and the sunshine seemed to fade. There was no mother to run to, no one to tell him where he might find her, only the strange sad words which he could not understand when they told him she was dead.

It was sad for little Hugh, but it was sadder still for his father, and the lord of Avalon felt he could no longer live in the castle that was now so dark and cheerless. So his thoughts turned towards a house close by where men lived together who wished to serve God, and he determined to spend the rest of his life with them. Hugh was only eight years old, too young to be left behind, so together the father and little son entered the priory, and left the castle and lands of Avalon to the elder sons.

It seemed strange for such a child to share the solemn strict life of these servants of God, but his father was glad it should be so. "I will have him taught to carry on warfare for God before he learns to live for the world," he said, as he looked at the well-knit straight little figure with the fearless eyes, every inch a soldier's son. Then little Hugh squared his shoulders and gazed proudly into his father's face. He scarcely understood what it all meant, but he loved the sound of those warlike words, "the warfare of God."

Among all those grave and learned men the child might perhaps have been spoilt, for he had a wonderfully winning way and a keen love of fun, while he was so quick to learn, and had such a marvellous memory, that it was a pleasure to teach him. But the brothers were too kind to spoil the child, and the old chronicle tells us "his infant body was made familiar with the scourge of the pedagogue."

There was a school at Grenoble, close by, to which Hugh was sent, and there he soon became a great favourite. He was eager at games as well as at lessons, and excelled in both. But his father, watching him, would sometimes disapprove of too many games, and would remind him of that "warfare of God."

"Little Hugh, little Hugh," he said, "I am bringing thee up for Christ. Sports are not thy business." Then he would tell him the story of other boys who had been brought up to serve God; about Samuel, who had heard God's voice because he listened so eagerly; of David, who learned to do things thoroughly, and to aim so straight at a mark that afterwards he could not fail to slay the giant and win a victory for the Lord.

So the boy grew into a youth, eager to begin the warfare for which his father had trained him. But there was other service awaiting him first close at home. His father was now growing old and infirm, and needed daily care and patient tending. With skilful gentle hands Hugh served him. Even the commonest duty was a pleasure to the son who so loved his father. He washed and dressed the old man, carried him in his strong young arms, prepared his food, counting each service an honour, as the service to a king. When his father's eyes grew dim, when his hands were frail and trembling, when his feet could no longer bear him, and the pleasant sounds of the busy world woke no echo in his dull ears, Hugh was eyes and hands, feet and ears, giving above all a willing service. Many a lesson had the father taught his child in the days of his strength, but the best of all lessons he taught in the days of his weakness—the lesson of loving patient service. So the old man lived to bless the son whom he had trained for God, and that blessing was like a spring of living water in Hugh's heart. Long after, when many troubles came, and the saint had travelled far along the hot and dusty road of life, he told a friend how the remembrance of his father's blessing was like a cup of cool water which he loved to "draw up thirstily from his eager heart."

That service ended, Hugh's thoughts began to turn to the warfare of which he had always dreamed. He had already been ordained, and his preaching stirred the people, but he longed for some harder duties and a sterner life.

Far away among the heights of the snow-capped mountains, there was a house of holy men just gathered together by Saint Brune. It was called the Great Chartreuse, and there the monks lived almost like hermits. They had little cells cut out of the bare rock, and their dress was a white sheep-skin with a hair-shirt beneath. On Sundays they each received a loaf of bread, which was to last all the week for their food, and although they had their meals together, they ate in strict silence, for no one was allowed to talk.

This was surely a place where one might endure hardness, and Hugh desired eagerly to join the brotherhood. Perhaps, too, he felt that he would be living nearer heaven up there amongst the snowy peaks.

But the prior looked somewhat scornfully at the young eager face.

"The men who inhabit these rocks," he said, "are hard as the rocks themselves, severe to themselves and others."

That was exactly what Hugh was longing for, and made him desire more than ever to enter the service, and although there were many difficulties in the way, he persevered steadfastly, and at last was received as a Carthusian monk.

Like all the other brothers, he lived, of course, a silent solitary life, but for him there were friends and companions which were not recognised in the monastery. He had always loved birds and beasts, and in this quiet life he found they were quick to make friends with him. Little by little he learned their secrets and their ways, and taught them to love and trust him. When he sat down to supper, his friends the birds would come hopping and fluttering in, ready to share his meal, perching on his finger and pecking the food from his spoon. Then from the woods the shy squirrels came flitting in, looking at him boldly with their bright inquiring eyes, while they made themselves quite at home, and whisked the food from his very plate with saucy boldness. Life could never be very lonely for Hugh with such a crowd of companions.

Meanwhile, in the little grey island of the north, better days were dawning, and with the death of King Stephen, law and order began once more to be restored. Henry II. ruled with a firmer hand, and the fear of God, and the desire to serve Him, awoke again in men's hearts. Throughout the land many churches were built, and many a battle was fought for the right. Thomas à Becket, the Archbishop of Canterbury, so foully murdered in his own cathedral, gave up his life willingly "in the name of Christ, and for the defence of the Church," and his example roused the people to insist that God's house and God's servants should be properly respected.

The King himself, sorrowfully repentant of his share in the murder of the Archbishop, made a vow to found three abbeys, and invited monks from the monasteries abroad to come and settle in them.

Now one of the places chosen by the King for founding an abbey was Witham in Gloucester, but instead of building a proper home for the monks, Henry merely seized the land from the poor peasants without paying for it, and without finding them other homes. Of course the abbey did not flourish. The first abbot would not stay and the second died, and it seemed as if it was to be quite a failure, until the King thought of sending to the monastery of the Great Chartreuse to ask for an abbot who would rule with a strong arm and help to found a brotherhood.

"We must send our best," said the prior; and when he said that, all the monks knew that Hugh of Avalon would be chosen. Strong and steadfast as the rocks amongst which he dwelt, he was as fearless and brave as a lion, and yet with a heart so gentle and tender that all weak and helpless creatures loved and trusted him.

So it was that Hugh of Avalon came to England, and we may claim him as one of our own saints.

As soon as the new abbot found out how unjustly the King had dealt with the peasants of Witham, he set about to put things right.

"My lord," he said to the King, "until the last penny is paid to these poor men, the place cannot be given to us."

It was little wonder that from the beginning the poor people loved and respected their abbot, and his justice and fearlessness won the King's friendship too. There was no one Henry cared to consult more than this new friend of his, who was never afraid of telling him the truth.

When some time had passed, and the monks' houses still remained unbuilt, three of the brothers went to remind the King of his broken promises.

"You think it a great thing to give us bread which we do not need," said one of the brothers, who was very angry. "We will leave your kingdom, and depart to our desert Chartreuse and our rocky Alps."

The King turned to Hugh.

"Will you also depart?" he asked.

"My lord," said Hugh quietly, "I do not despair of you. Rather I pity your hindrances and occupations which weigh against the care of your soul. You are busy, but when God will help, you will finish the good work you have begun."

"By my soul," cried the King, "while I breathe thou shalt not leave my kingdom. With thee I will share my counsels, with thee also the necessary care of my soul."

So the monastery was built, and the King's friendship for the abbot increased. It happened just at that time also that, as Henry was crossing to Normandy, the ship in which he sailed came nigh to being wrecked by a great gale that swept suddenly down upon her. The King in his fear prayed to God to save him for the sake of the good deeds and holy life of his friend the abbot. Then as the storm sank and the ship reached land, Henry felt sure he owed his safety to that good man. The country people, too, were fond of talking of the miracles worked by their beloved abbot, but Hugh himself would not hear of them. In the lives of the saints it was the miracles he counted least of all.

"The holiness of the saints," he would say, "was the greatest miracle and the best example for us to follow. Those who look at outward miracles through the little doors of their eyes, often see nothing by the inward gaze of faith."

It was a very different life at Witham to the hermit life among the snowy mountains, but Hugh remained just the same simple steadfast man. He still wore the rough hair-shirt and ate the same poor fare, and here as in his rocky cell the birds flew in to make friends with him and eat from his plate.

But after eleven quiet years at Witham, Hugh was called to harder work, for it was decided to make him Bishop of Lincoln. It was sorely against his will that he accepted the honour, and it was with a heavy heart that he bade farewell to the quiet monastery life.

There was great excitement and delight, however, among the company that attended the abbot on his way to Lincoln. The canons wore their richest cloaks, and the gilded trappings of their horses made a brave show as they clattered along. But all their grandeur could not hide that one shabby figure in their midst. Hugh, clothed in his monk's robe, rode on his old mule, and behind him was strapped a large bundle of bedding, sheep-skins, and rugs.

"Dost see our abbot?" said one to another. "He will put us all to shame. Men will laugh at the sight of the new bishop riding thus, with his old baggage strapped behind."

It was useless to suggest that the servants should take charge of the bundle. Hugh plodded on, too busy with his thoughts to notice the shame and discomfort of his companions.

At last, when twilight had fallen and night was coming on, one of his friends thought of a plan to save their dignity. One of the servants stole up softly from behind and cut the straps which bound the heavy sheep-skin bundle, so that it slipped off and was carried away to be placed among the other baggage, while Hugh went jogging on, dreaming his dreams and thinking little of earthly matters.

There was no thought of personal grandeur in Hugh's heart. Rather he felt like a sailor setting out on a perilous voyage, with storm-clouds already brooding close above the waves of this troublesome world. He walked barefooted to the cathedral where he was enthroned, clad only in his monk's robe. He was a strange shabby figure indeed among those gorgeous churchmen, but he walked with the bearing of a soldier and the dignity of a king.

At his palace of Stow the Bishop found a new friend ready to welcome him, one of the kind of friends he specially loved. In the lake among the woods a wild swan had been seen to swoop down and take up its abode. It was so large and strong that it easily drove away or killed all the tame swans there, and then triumphantly beat the air with its great white wings over its new dominions, and cried aloud with a harsh shrill voice.

It seemed willing to be friendly with the servants, although it would allow no one to touch it, so with some difficulty it was enticed into the palace to be shown to the Lord-Bishop. Hugh, with his love for animals, soon made friends, and the swan came closer and closer, until it took some bread from his hand, and from that moment adopted him as a friend and master. It was frightened of nothing as long as Hugh was at hand, and it became so fiercely loving that no one dared come near the Bishop while the swan was on guard. Sometimes when he was asleep, and it was needful for his servants to pass his bed to fetch something that was wanted, they dared not go near him, for the swan would spread its great snowy white wings in defence, looking like a very angry guardian angel, and if they came nearer, would threaten them with its strong beak. Harsh and disdainful to every one else, the curious creature was always gentle and loving towards Hugh, and would often nestle its head and long neck up his wide sleeve, and lay its head upon his breast, uttering soft little cries of pleasure. When the Bishop was away from home, the swan would never enter the palace, but even before his return was expected by others, there was a sound of a great beating of wings and strange cries from the lake among the woods.

"Now hark ye," the country people would say, "surely our Lord-Bishop is returning home. Dost thou not hear that strange bird preparing his welcome?"

No sooner did the luggage carts and servants begin to arrive than the swan would leave the lake and make its way with great long strides into the palace. The moment it heard its master's voice it ran to him, swelling its throat with great cries of welcome, and following at his heels wherever he went. Only at the end, when the Bishop's life was near its close and he came to Stow for the last time, his favourite had no welcome for him. Hiding itself

SAINT HUGH OF LINCOLN

SAINT HUGH AND THE WHITE SWAN

among the reeds, it hung its head, and had all the ways of a sick creature. In some strange way it seemed to know that it was to lose its master, and the shadow of his coming death seemed already to have fallen upon it.

People have wondered much at this curious friendship between Saint Hugh and the white swan, but they forget that for those of His servants who love and serve Him, God has said, "I will make a covenant for them with the beasts of the field and with the fowls of heaven, and with the creeping things of the ground."

Troubles soon began for the Bishop in his new life. He had a keen sense of justice, and could not bear to see the weak treated unfairly by the strong, and one of his first acts was to punish the King's own chief forester for oppressing the poor.

That was a bold act, but worse was to follow when the new Bishop refused to give a place in the cathedral stalls to one of the King's favourite courtiers.

"The stalls are for priests, and not for courtiers," was the message he sent to Henry. "The King has plenty of rewards for those who fight his battles. Let him not take their offices from those who serve the King of Kings."

Henry was both hurt and angry, and ordered that the Bishop should come at once to him at Woodstock.

"He is both ungrateful and troublesome," said the King. "I will speak with him myself."

It was a sunny summer day when Hugh arrived at Woodstock, and he was told that the King was awaiting his arrival in one of the cool forest glades. There, under the trees, upon the green sward among a company of courtiers, sat the King in a leafy bower. The sunbeams filtered through the interwoven branches and threw patches of gold upon the green, while the birds in the boughs overhead sang in royal concert. But the song of the birds was the only sound that broke the stillness. The King and his courtiers sat sternly silent, and never a figure moved nor a word of welcome was spoken when the Bishop came through the trees.

"Good morrow, your Majesty," said Hugh.

There was no answer. Every one sat silent, and no one as much as glanced at the Bishop. At length the King looked up and asked one of the attendants for a needle and thread. He had hurt one of his fingers, and the rag around it was loose. Very solemnly he began to sew, stitch, stitch, stitch, in unbroken silence, while the sunbeams danced and the birds sang.

A smile at last dawned on Hugh's face, for he began to guess what the silence meant. He was surprised, but not in the least afraid. Going round to where the King sat, he put both hands on the shoulders of the man who was sitting next to Henry and gently moved him to one side. Then he sat down in the vacant place, and with a mirthful look in his eyes, watched the King as he sewed in gloomy silence.

"How like your Highness is to your kinsfolk of Falaise," said the Bishop thoughtfully.

The King tried to look dignified, then stopped his stitching, and burst out into a peal of laughter, rolling from side to side. The rest of the company were much amazed, but as soon as the King could speak he explained the joke.

"Know you," he said, "what sort of an insult this strange fellow has offered to us? I will explain it to you. Our great ancestor Duke William, the conqueror of this land, was born of a mother of no very high extraction, who belonged to a town in Normandy, namely Falaise. This town is very celebrated for its skill in leather-stitching. When, then, this scoffer saw me stitching my finger, straightway he declared me to be like the tanners of Falaise, and one of their kinsmen."

The Bishop's fearlessness and the good joke put Henry in a better temper, and he listened quietly to what Hugh had to say.

"I know well, sire," said the Bishop earnestly, "that you took great pains to get me made a bishop, and I would in return do my best to prove your choice a wise one. I acted justly in these matters, and because my actions were right I felt sure you would approve them."

The King nodded his head, and once more the Bishop's faith in him met its reward. The forester

SAINT HUGH OF LINCOLN

was ordered to be flogged, and never again while Hugh was bishop did any courtier apply for a stall in the cathedral.

Many a time in after days did Hugh cross the royal will and fall under the King's displeasure, but he never swerved from the right, and faced the royal wrath so fearlessly, that in the end he earned for himself the title of the "Hammer of Kings."

All the clergy and the poor around loved their Bishop. Every one in trouble, the poor and the sick, came to him for help, and no one ever came in vain. But perhaps it was the children whom he specially loved. To people who did not understand that love, it seemed almost like a miracle to see how children were drawn towards him. Little faces brightened into smiles when they saw him; little sun-browned hands caught at his cloak as he passed, happy only if they might touch his robe. Even the babies, meeting his smile, stretched out their arms to go to him. It seemed as if he possessed some secret talisman to win their hearts. A miraculous secret the wise people called it, but children knew it was no secret at all, but just the old miracle of love.

Perhaps the saddest of all God's creatures in those days were the poor lepers, who lived apart and were shunned by every one because of their terrible sickness. And just because they were so sad and suffering, the good Bishop loved to go to them and try to help and comfort them. Through the sunny world of light and laughter these poor lepers passed along like gaunt grey shadows, with the one dreadful cry upon their lips, "Unclean, unclean." Men and women drew back shuddering when the grey shadows passed by, warned by the harsh clang of the lepers' bell. Even children hid their faces in terror, and though some kind hearts would give them food and help, there was no kind hand that would venture to touch the leper.

But Hugh had no fear of the sickness and no horror of these poor souls. His Master's touch had healed many such an one in days gone by, and he felt that in touching them he "touched the hand of Him who touched the leper of old in Galilee." Gently and lovingly the Bishop tended the poor outcasts. He fed and clothed them, washed their weary painful feet, and often stooping down, he kissed their poor scarred cheeks. Perhaps above all it was the human touch they longed for, and looking into his kind eyes, they would have some faint idea of the wondrous love which the lepers of old had seen in the pitying eyes of our dear Lord Himself.

"Surely this is too much," said his clergy, watching their Bishop with shuddering glances. "What good can it do? We know of course that Saint Martin, of blessed memory, healed the leper with his kiss, but the miracle does not happen now."

The Bishop only looked at them with a quiet smile.

"Martin by his kiss brought bodily health to the leper," he said, "but the leper by his kiss brings health to my soul."

SAINT HUGH OF LINCOLN

It was men's bodies as well as their souls that Hugh cared for, and it vexed him sorely to see how carelessly the poor bodies were treated when the souls had gone home to God. No matter how busy he was, he would put everything aside to pay the last honours to the dead. Once, on his way to dine with the King, he found the body of a poor beggar lying by the wayside, and at once stopped to bury it. Messengers came to bid him come at once, as the King was furious at his delay, but the Bishop went on calmly with his work and bade them tell the King he need not wait for him. "I am occupied in the service of the King of Kings," he said: "I cannot neglect it."

Very soon after King Henry's death, trouble arose between the Bishop and the new King Richard. He of the lion heart could not understand how one of his own subjects dare disobey his orders, and when the Bishop of Lincoln refused to make the clergy pay to provide soldiers for foreign service, he ordered him to come and explain his disobedience in person.

Hugh started at once for France, where the King awaited his coming near Rouen. Richard was in the chapel, seated upon his royal throne, and the service had begun when the Bishop arrived. But Hugh went straight up to him and demanded the usual kiss. Richard answered never a word, but turned coldly away.

"Give me the kiss, my lord King," said Hugh, seizing the royal mantle and giving it a hearty shake.

"You do not deserve the kiss," said the King in a surly tone.

"Nay, but I do," answered Hugh, and he gave the robe a stronger shake, drawing it out as far as it would reach. "Give me the kiss."

King Richard was not at all accustomed to being shaken and spoken to in that tone of voice, but there was something about the man that even kings could not resist, and the kiss was given. Then Hugh went to kneel humbly in the lowest place in the chapel, until the service was over and he could explain why he had refused to send the money demanded of him. And not only did he convince the King of his justice, but he went on to calmly reprove Richard for some of his faults, and suggest many improvements in his behaviour. The King listened meekly, and was heard to say afterwards: "If all bishops were like my lord of Lincoln, not a prince among us could lift up his head against them."

Time passed on and Richard died. Then John, the false and mean, reigned over England, and many a warning word did he hear from the lips of the good Bishop. But Hugh was nearing the end of his journey now, and with a thankful heart he prepared to lay down his arms after his long warfare in the service of God.

In the house belonging to the see of Lincoln at the old Temple, the faithful soldier and servant lay awaiting the messenger of the King of Kings.

"Prepare some ashes," he directed, "and spread them on the bare ground, in the form of a cross, and lay me there to die."

The weary body, clad in the rough hair-shirt, was laid on the cross, and, as the grey shadows of twilight gathered in the quiet room, the strains of the evening hymn came floating through the open window.

"Lord, now lettest Thou Thy servant depart in peace," chanted the choristers of Saint Paul's, and even as they sang, the prayer was answered. Only the worn-out body lay upon the cross of ashes; the soul had indeed departed in peace, and the warfare of the faithful soldier was accomplished.

They carried the saint's body to Lincoln, and the whole countryside, rich and poor, high and low, came out to meet him, while King John and William of Scotland shared the honour of bearing him to his last resting-place.

"It may be observed," says the old chronicle, "that he who neglected kings to bury the dead, at his own burial was followed by kings."

The loving memory of Saint Hugh has faded and grown dim, perhaps, with passing years, but at Lincoln the great cathedral, which he helped to build with his own hands, speaks still in its strength and beauty of the bishop-saint, so strong in his steadfast courage, so beautiful in his tender love for the weak and helpless of the earth.

Lightning Source UK Ltd.
Milton Keynes UK
UKHW041430010719
345364UK00002B/657/P